Compendium of the History of Rome

Marcus Velleius Paterculus

Works of the Public Domain

TABLE OF CONTENTS

BOOK I

I. Cities founded by the Greeks on their return from Troy; acts of Orestes; arrival of Tyrrhenus in Italy

II. Return of the Heraclidæ; death of Codrus; founding of Megara, Gades, and Utica.

III. Of the Achæans, Pelasgi, Thessalians, and the settlement of Corinth

IV. Chalcis, Magnesia, Cumæ, Naples, and many other cities, founded

V. Age and character of Homer

VI. Of the Assyrian empire, Lycurgus, and the origin of Carthage

VII. Of Hesiod, and the building of Capua and Nola

VIII. The Olympic games; the founding of Rome

IX. The second Macedonian war

X. Of Antiochus the Great, and Æmilius Paulus

XI. Pseudo-Philippus; Metellus Macedonicus

XII. Destruction of Corinth and Carthage

XIII. Death of Cato; characters of Mummius and Scipio Africanus

XIV-XV. Establishment of Roman colonies

XVI-XVII. Considerations why many eminent men, in the several arts, arise at the same time

XVIII. Commencement of similar observations on cities.

BOOK II

I. Declension of Roman virtue after the destruction of Carthage; wars with Viriathus and Numantia

II-III. Acts and death of Tiberius Gracchus

IV. Aristonicus defeated; Numantia overthrown; character and death of Publius Scipio

V. Acts of Aulus Brutus in Spain

VI. Proceedings and death of Caius Gracchus

VII. Cruelty of Opimius

VIII. Narbo Martius founded; Cato condemned for extortion; triumphs of the Metelli and Minutius

IX. Eminent Roman orators and writers

X. Severity of the censors; family of the Domitii

XI-XII. The Jugurthine war; the acts of Marius

XIII-XIV. Ill-fortune and death of Drusus

XV-XVI. The colony of Carthage; the Italian war

XVII. The civic franchise granted to the Italians; character of Sylla

XVIII. War with Mithridates commenced; acts of Sulpicius

XIX. Civil war between Marius and Sylla

XX. The consul Pompeius murdered by the soldiers; proceedings of Cinna

XXI. Cinna succeeds in recalling Marius

XXII. Marius's proscription

XXIII. Marius's death; success of Sylla against Mithridates

XXIV. Deaths of Fimbria, Lucilius, and Cinna

XXV-XXVI. Further proceedings of Sylla

XXVII. Fate of Pontius Telesinus, and of the younger Marius

XXVIII. Sylla's dictatorship and proscription

XXIX. Character of Pompey, afterwards called the Great

XXX. Death of Sertorius; triumphs of Metellus and Pompey; war with Spartacus

XXXI-XXXII. Pompey suppresses the pirates

XXXIII. Pompey receives the command of the Mithridatic war; acts of Lucullus

XXXIV. Conquest of Crete; conspiracy of Catiline

XXXV. Character of Cato; deaths of Catiline and the other conspirators

XXXVI. Augustus Cæsar born; learned men of that age

XXXVII. Tigranes surrenders to Pompey

XXXVIII-XXXIX. Names of Roman provinces, and by whom conquered

XL. Pompey conquers Mithridates, and triumphs

XLI-XLIII. Descent, character, and actions of Julius Cæsar

XLIV. First Triumvirate; consulship of Cæsar

XLV. Of Clodius, Cicero, and Cato

XLVI. Cæsar's acts in Gaul; Crassus killed in Parthia

XLVII. Further proceedings of Cæsar; Clodius slain by Milo

XLVIII-LII. Civil war between Cæsar and Pompey

LIII. Death of Pompey

LIV-LV. Cæsar's actions in Egypt, Africa, and Spain

LVI-LVII. Cæsar's triumphs and death

LVIII. Proceedings of Brutus and Cicero

LIX. Opening of Cæsar's will; family and character of Augustus

LX-LXI. Dissensions and war between Cæsar and Antony

LXII Provinces decreed to Brutus and Cassius by the senate; Cæsar slighted

LXIII. Antony joins the army of Lepidus

LXIV. Death of Decimus Brutus; banishment of Cicero

LXV. The second Triumvirate

LXVI. Another proscription; death of Cicero

LXVII. Conduct of the Romans at the time of the proscription

LXVIII. Of Cælius and Milo; of the clemency of Cæsar

LXIX. Of Dolabella, Vatinius, and the Pædian law

LXX. Proceedings of Brutus and Cassius; they are slain in the battle of Philippi

LXXI-LXXII. Consequences of the battle

LXXIII. Of Sextus Pompeius

LXXIV-LXXV. Of Antony, Cæsar, and Livia

LXXVI. Of Caius Velleius and Fulvia; peace between Cæsar and Antony

LXXVII. Peace with Sextus Pompeius

LXXVIII. Antony marries Octavia, Cæsar's sister; Labienus overthrown

LXXIX. War resumed with Sextus Pompeius; Cæsar marries Livia

LXXX. Degradation of Lepidus

LXXXI. Cæsar suppresses a mutiny in the army

LXXXII. Antony invades Parthia

LXXXIII. Of Plancus

LXXXIV-LXXXVI. Battle of Actium, and what immediately followed it

LXXXVII. Death of Antony

LXXXVIII. Conspiracy, death, and character of Lepidus

LXXXIX. Cæsar's triumphs and plans of government

XC. Reduction of Spain and Dalmatia

XCI. Roman ensigns recovered from the Parthians

XCII. Of Sentius Saturninus

XCIII. Of Marcellus and Agrippa

XCIV-XCVII. Expeditions of Tiberius and Drusus; death of Drusus

XCVIII. The Thracian war—XCIX. Tiberius retires to Rhodes

C. Hostilities resumed in Parthia and Germany; excesses of Julia

CI-CII. Caius Cæsar in Parthia; his death

CIII-CIV. Tiberius and Agrippa adopted by Augustus

CV-CIX. Acts of Tiberius in Germany

CX. Insurrection in Dalmatia

CXI-CXV. Proceedings of Tiberius against the Dalmatians and Pannonians; both are subdued

CXVI. Of some who were distinguished in this war

CXVII. Loss of the legions in Germany under Varus

CXVIII-CXIX. Of Arminius; death of Varus

CXX-CXXII. Tiberius conducts the German war; his triumphs

CXXIII. Death of Augustus

CXXIV. Tiberius succeeds him

CXXV. Mutiny in Germany and Illyricum suppressed

CXXVI. Government of Tiberius

CXXVII-CXXVIII. Of Sejanus

CXXIX-CXXX. Observations on Tiberius

CXXXI. Prayer for the prosperity of Rome.

BOOK I

I

* * * * [Epeus,] being parted[1] by a storm from Nestor his commander, built Metapontum[2]. Teucer, not being received at home by his father Telamon, for his pusillanimity in not avenging the injustice shown to his brother[3], sailed to Cyprus, where he built Salamis, a city named after his own birthplace. Pyrrhus, the son of Achilles, took possession of Epirus, and Phidippus[4] of Ephyra in Thesprotia. As to Agamemnon, the king of kings, he was driven by a tempest on the island of Crete, where he founded three cities, Mycenæ, Tegea, and Pergamus, of which two had named from his own country, and the third from the recollection of his recent victory. Soon after, being entrapped by the treachery of his cousin[5] Ægisthus, who bore a hereditary hatred towards him, and by the malice of his wife, he was murdered. Ægisthus held the throne for seven years; when Orestes, in concert with his sister Electra, a woman of masculine courage, and sharer in all his designs, slew both Ægisthus and his own mother. That his deed was approved by the gods, was apparent from the length of his life and the prosperity of his reign; for he lived ninety years and reigned seventy. He also revenged himself on Pyrrhus, son of Achilles, with similar spirit; for Pyrrhus having supplanted him by marrying Hermione, the daughter of Menelaus and Helen, who had been betrothed to Orestes, Orestes slew him at Delphi.

During this period, the brothers Lydus and Tyrrhenus, who reigned in Lydia, were compelled, by the unproductiveness of their corn-fields, to cast lots which of the two, taking half of the people with him, should quit their country. The lot fell upon Tyrrhenus[6], who, sailing into Italy, gave, from his own name, an illustrious and enduring appellation to the country, its inhabitants, and the adjacent sea. After the death of Orestes, his sons, Penthilus and Tisamenus, reigned three years.

II

At this time, about eighty years after Troy was taken, and a hundred and twenty after the translation of Hercules to the gods, the family of Pelops, which, after expelling the Heraclidæ, had held, during the whole of this period, the sovereignty of the Peloponnesus, was in turn expelled by them. The leaders in recovering the dominion were Temenus, Cresphontes, and Aristodemus, of whom Hercules was great-grandfather.

About the same period, Athens ceased to be ruled by kings, its last monarch being Codrus, the son of Melanthus, a man deserving of particular notice; for when the Spartans were severely pressing the Athenians in war, and Apollo had given an oracle that that side would be victorious whose leader should be killed by the enemy, Codrus, having laid aside his royal apparel, put on the attire of a shepherd, and went into the midst of the enemy's camp, where, intentionally provoking a quarrel, he was slain without being known[7]. From his death, eternal glory accrued to Codrus, and victory to the Athenians. Who can help admiring a man that sought for death with the same stratagems with which, by those of meaner spirit, life is wont to be sought? His son Medon was the first archon at Athens; from whom his descendants were called by the Athenians Medontidæ; and these, as well as the following archons, down to the time of Charops, held their office during life. The Peloponnesians, on retiring from the Athenian territory, founded Megara, a city equally distant from Corinth and Athens. At this time, also, a fleet of the Tyrians, then very powerful at sea, founded the city of Gades, on the remotest coast of Spain, at the extremity of one part of the world, and on an island surrounded by the Ocean, divided from the continent only by a very narrow strait. By the same people, also, a few years afterwards, Utica, in Africa, was

1

built. The children of Orestes, being expelled by the Heraclidæ, and harassed by various misfortunes, as well as by hardships at sea, found a settlement, in the fifteenth year after their expulsion, opposite the island of Lesbos.

III

During this period Greece was shaken by violent commotions. The Achæans, driven from Laconia, settled in those tracts which they now occupy. The Pelasgi removed to Athens; and a young man of warlike spirit, by name Thessalus, and by birth a Thesprotian, took forcible possession, with the aid of a numerous body of his countrymen, of that region which is now, from his name, called Thessaly, but which was before termed the country of the Myrmidons. Hence there is reason to wonder at those authors, who, in their accounts of the Trojan period, speak of that country by the name of Thessaly; a fault which not only other writers commit, but writers of tragedy more frequently than any; though in them, least of all, is such licence to be excused, for they express nothing in their own character of poets, but narrate everything under the persons of those who lived at the time. But if any one shall maintain that they were called Thessalians from Thessalus, the son of Hercules[8], he will have to give a reason why the people did not assume this name till the time of the latter Thessalus. A little before this, Aletes, sixth in descent from Hercules, and son of Hippotes, rebuilt[9] Corinth on the Isthmus, which was previously called Ephyre, and which forms the principal barrier of the Peloponnesus. Nor is there any reason for us to wonder that it was called Corinth by Homer; for, in his character of poet, he calls both this city, and some of the Ionian colonies, built long after the taking of Troy, by the same names which they bore in his own times.

IV

The Athenians settled colonies at Chalcis and Eretria in Eubœa; the Lacedæmonians established another at Magnesia in Asia. Not long afterwards, the people of Chalcis, who were sprung, as I have just said, from the Athenians, founded Cumæ in Italy, under the leadership of Hippocles and Megasthenes. The course of their fleet was directed, as some say, by the flight of a dove that preceded it, or, as others state, by the sound of brazen instruments during the night, such as is commonly made at the rites of Ceres. Some natives of this city, a long time after, built Neapolis; and the exemplary fidelity of both these cities to the Romans, renders them eminently worthy of their high reputation, and of the delightful situations which they enjoy. But the institutions of their original country have been more diligently preserved by the Neapolitans; for the neighbourhood of the Osci altered the manners of the people of Cumæ. The present extent of the walls of these cities shows the greatness of their power in former days.

At a subsequent period, a vast number of Grecian youth, seeking, from a redundance of population, for new settlements, poured into Asia. The Ionians, sailing from Athens under the conduct of Ion, took possession of the finest part of the sea-coast, now called Ionia, and built the cities of Ephesus, Miletus, Colophon, Priene, Lebedus, Myus, Erythra, Clazomenæ, and Phocæa. They also seized on many of the island in the Ægean and Icarian seas, as Samos, Chios, Andros, Tenos, Paros, Delos, and others of less note. Soon after, the Æolians also, setting out from Greece, and wandering about for a long time, found at length settlements not less valuable, and founded some famous cities, as Smyrna, Cyme, Larissa, Myrina, and Mitylene, with others in the island of Lesbos.

V

It was at this time that the illustrious genius of Homer shone forth; a genius great beyond example; for by the grandeur of his subjects, and the splendour of his verse, he has gained an exclusive right[10] to the name of poet. What is most remarkable with respect to him, is, that neither was there any one before him whom he could imitate, nor has any one since been found who could imitate him. Nor can we point to any other author, except Homer and Antilochus, who arrived at the highest excellence in the kind of writing of which he was the inventor. He lived longer after the Trojan war, which he took for his subject, than some suppose; for he flourished about nine hundred and fifty years ago, and was born within a thousand. It is not at all surprising, therefore, that he frequently uses the expression οἷοι νῦν βροτοί εἰσι, such as men now are; for by this the difference in mankind, as well as in age, is signified. Whoever believes that he was born blind, must be himself deprived of all his senses.

VI

In the subsequent period, about eight hundred and seventy years ago, the empire of Asia was transferred from the Assyrians, who had held it a thousand and seventy years, to the Medes. For Arbaces, a Mede, dethroned and put to death their monarch Sardanapalus, a man immersed in luxurious gratifications, and courting extravagant pleasures to his own destruction; and who was the thirty-third in succession from Ninus and Semiramis, the founders of Babylon, a succession so regular that the son had in every instance inherited the throne of his father.

In this age, too, Lycurgus, the Lacedæmonian, a man of royal birth, was the author of a most severe and just body of laws, and of a system of education most suitable[11] to the character of his countrymen; and Sparta, as long as she adhered to it, was eminently prosperous.

During the same period, sixty-five years before the foundation of Rome, the city of Carthage was built by Elissa of Tyre, whom some suppose to be the same as Dido. About the same time, Caranus, a man of regal extraction, being the sixteenth in descent from Hercules, took his departure from Argos, and seized on the kingdom of Macedonia. The great Alexander, being the seventeenth in succession from Caranus, might justly boast of his lineages, as being on his mother's side from Achilles, and on his father's from Hercules[12].

VII

Coeval with these events, and separated by about a hundred and twenty years from Homer, lived Hesiod, a man of exquisite taste, remarkable for the gentle sweetness of his numbers, and a great lover of ease and retirement. As he was nearest in time to his illustrious predecessor, he was also nearest in the reputation of his writings. He avoided resembling Homer in one respect, for he has mentioned both his country and his parents; but the former in the bitterest terms of reproach, on account of a fine which it had imposed upon him.

While I am treating of foreign matters, a point in our own history occurs to me, which has given rise to many mistakes, and about which there is the greatest discrepancy in the opinions of writers. Some authors say that, during this period, about eight hundred and thirty years ago, Capua and Nola were founded by the Tuscans; and to their opinion I readily assent. But how greatly does Marcus Cato differ from them, who states that "Capua was first founded by the Tuscans, and Nola some time afterwards; but that Capua had stood, before it was taken by the Romans, about two hundred and sixty years." If this be the case, and as only two hundred and forty years have elapsed since the taking of Capua, it can be but five hundred years since it was built. For my own part, speaking with deference to the accuracy of Cato, I can scarcely believe that so great a city rose, flourished, fell, and sprung up again, in so short a space of time.

VIII

The Olympic games, the most celebrated of all spectacles of entertainment, and best adapted for invigorating the mind and the body, had their commencement soon afterwards, the founder of them being Iphitus of Elis, who instituted these contests, as well as a market, eight hundred and four years before you, Marcus Vinicius, entered upon your consulship. By some, however, Atreus is said to have commenced this solemnity, when he exhibited, in this same place, funeral games in honour of his father Pelops, about twelve hundred and fifty years ago, on which occasion Hercules was victor in every kind of contest.

It was at this time that the archons at Athens ceased to be elected for life, Alcmæon being the last that was so appointed, and were chosen only for ten years; an arrangement which lasted for seventy years, when the administration was committed to annual magistrates. Of those who held office for ten years, the first was Charops, and the last was Eryxias; of those who retained it but one year, the first was Creon.

In the sixth Olympiad, twenty-two years from the commencement of the first, Romulus, the son of Mars, having avenged the wrong done to his grandfather, founded the city of Rome on the Palatine hill, on the day of the feast of Pales[13]; from which time, to that of your consulate, is a period of seven hundred and eighty-three years. This event took place four hundred and thirty-seven years after the taking of Troy. The work was effected by Romulus, with the assistance of the Latin legions of his grandfather; for I can readily believe those who give this account, since, without such assistance, and with merely a defenceless band of shepherds, he could hardly have established a new city, while the Vejentines, the other Etruscans, and the Sabines, were so close upon him, how much soever he strengthened it by opening an asylum being the two groves. He had a hundred chosen men, called Fathers, as a public council. Such origin had the term Patricians[14]. The seizure of the Sabine virgins * * * * * * * * * * * * * * *

IX

* * * proved a more powerful enemy[15] than the Romans had apprehended; for he maintained a struggle, during two years, with such variation of fortune, that he had generally the advantage, and drew a great part of Greece into alliance with him. Even the Rhodians, who had previously been most faithful to the Romans, began, with wavering allegiance, to watch the turns of fortune, and appeared rather inclined to the side of the king. Eumenes, too, in this war, was undecided in his views, and acted consistently neither with his brother's[16] proceedings at first, nor with his own general conduct. At length the senate and people of Rome elected to the consulship Lucius Æmilius Paulus, who had previously triumphed both as prætor and consul; a man deserving of the highest honour which merit can be conceived to attain. He was the son of that Paulus who commenced with such reluctance the battle of Cannæ, so fatal to the commonwealth, and who met death in it with so much fortitude. He routed Perses, in a great battle, near a city named Pydna in Macedonia, and drove him from his camp; and at last, after destroying his troops, forced him to flee from his dominions. The king, after quitting Macedonia, took refuge in the island of Samothrace, and committed himself, as a suppliant, to the sanctuary of the temple. Cnæus Octavius, the prætor, who had the command of the fleet, followed him thither, and prevailed on him, rather by persuasion than by force, to trust himself to the honour of the Romans.

Æmilius Paulus, in consequence, led this most eminent and celebrated prince in triumph.

In this year, too, were two other famous triumphs; that of Octavius, the naval commander, and that of Anicius, who drove before his chariot Gentius the king of the Illyrians. How constantly envy attends eminent fortune, and how closely it pursues the highest characters, may be understood from the follow circumstance, that while no one objected to the triumphs of Anicius and Octavius, there were some who endeavoured to hinder that of Paulus, though it far exceeded the others, as well in the greatness of Perses as a monarch, as in the magnificent display of war-trophies, and the quantity of money carried in it; as it brought into the treasury two hundred thousand sestertia[17], being beyond comparison more splendid than any triumph that preceded it.

X

During the same time, while Antiochus Epiphanes, who built the Temple of Jupiter at Athens, and who was then king of Syria, was besieging Ptolemy the young king of Egypt, in Alexandria, Marcus Popilius Lænas was sent as ambassador to him, to require him to desist from the siege. Popilius delivered his message, and the king replying that he would consider of the matter, he drew a circle round him with a rod upon the sand, desiring him to give a decisive answer before he passed that boundary. Roman firmness overcame the king's hesitation, and the consul was obeyed.

Lucius Æmilius Paulus, who obtained the great victory over Perses, had four sons; of whom he had allowed the two eldest to be adopted, one by Publius Scipio, the son of Africanus, who retained nothing of his father's greatness but the splendour of his name and the force of his eloquence, and the other by Fabius Maximus; the two younger, at the time when he gained the victory, he had still at home, as being yet under age. Previously to the day of his triumph, when, according to ancient usage, he was making a statement of his services to an assembly without the city, he intreated the immortal gods, that if any of them looked enviously on his actions and fortune, they would vent their displeasure on himself rather than on the Commonwealth. This expression, as if uttered by an oracle, robbed him of a great part of his offspring; for of the two sons whom he had in his house, he lost one a few days before his triumph, and the other in fewer days after it.

About this time occurred the censorship of Fulvius Flaccus and Posthumius Albinus, which was exercised with great severity; for Cnæus Fulvius, the brother of Fulvius the censor, and partner with him in property[18], was expelled from the senate by those very censors.

XI

Subsequently to the conquest and capture of Perses, who died four years afterwards in private custody[19] at Alba, a man who, from his false representations concerning his birth, was called Pseudo-Philippus, (for he said that his name was Philip, and that he was of the royal blood, though he was, in reality, of the meanest extraction,) seized the government of Macedonia by force of arms, and assumed the ensigns of royalty. But he soon paid the penalty of his rashness; for the prætor Quintus Metellus, who, from his merit in war, had received the surname of Macedonicus, gained a noble victory over both the imposter and his nation, and subdued at the same time, in a great battle, the Achæans[20] who had recommenced hostilities. This is the Metellus Macedonicus who erected the porticos round the two temples without an inscription, now encircled by the porticos of Octavia, and who brought from Macedonia the group of equestrian statues that face the front of the temples, and form at present the chief ornament of the place. Of this group the following origin is related. Alexander the Great, it is said, desired Lysippus, an eminent artist in such performances, to make statues of such horsemen of his own troop as had fallen at the river Granicus, representing their likenesses in the figures, and placing one of Alexander himself among them. It was this Metellus, too, who first built at Rome a temple of marble[21], among the edifices just mentioned, and who was consequently the introducer of what is to be called either magnificence or luxury. It would be difficult to find, indeed, a man of any nation, age, or rank, whose felicity can be compared with that of Metellus; for besides his splendid triumph, his distinguished honours, his acknowledged pre-eminence in the state, his long extent of life, and his zealous yet harmless contests with opponents for the good of his country, he was the father of four sons, whom he saw arrive at manhood, and whom he left surviving, and in enjoyment of the highest honours. These four sons supported his bier before the Rostra, one of them having been consul and censor, another consul, the third being consul at the time, and the fourth a candidate for the honour, which he afterwards obtained. Such an end may rather be called a happy retirement from life, than death.

XII

The whole of Achaia, of which a great part had been reduced by the conduct and arms of Metellus, was now, as we have said, strongly inclined to hostilities, being instigated chiefly by the Corinthians, who were guilty even of great insults to the Romans; and to conduct the war against them the consul Mummius was chosen. About the same time, too, rather because the Romans wished to believe whatever was said against the Carthaginians, than because anything was said against them worthy of belief, the senate resolved on the destruction of Carthage. Accordingly Publius Scipio Æmilianus, a man who emulated alike the virtues of his grandfather Publius Africanus and his father Lucius Paulus; who, in every qualification for war or peace, was the most eminent of his age as well in natural ability as in acquired knowledge; who, through the whole of his life, neither did, nor said, nor thought anything but what was praiseworthy; and who, as I have observed, had been adopted by Scipio the son of Africanus, was elected consul, though at the time he was only candidate for an ædileship. He had been previously honoured in Spain with a mural, and in Africa with an obsidional crown; in Spain, also, in consequence of a challenge, he had, though but of moderate bodily strength, slain an antagonist of extraordinary stature; and he now pressed on the war against Carthage, which had been conducted for two years by the preceding consuls, with additional vigour. This city, which, rather from jealousy of its power than from any recent offence, was an object of hatred to Rome, he utterly destroyed, and made it as much a monument of his own military prowess as it had previously been of his grandfather's clemency.

Carthage was demolished a hundred and seventy-seven years ago, in the consulship of Cnæus Cornelius Lentulus and Lucius Mummius, after having stood six hundred and seventy-two years. Such was the end of Carthage, the rival of the empire of Rome, with which our forefathers commenced war in the consulate of Claudius and Fulvius, two hundred and ninety-six years before you, Marcus Vinicius, entered upon your consulship. Thus for a hundred and twenty years there subsisted between these two nations either war, or preparations for war, or unsettled peace. Nor did Rome, though the whole world were subdued, trust the she should be safe while there was left even the name of Carthage unremoved. So apt is hatred, arising from contentions, to continue longer than the fear of danger, and not to be laid aside even when the opposite party is vanquished; nor does the object of enmity cease to be detested until it has ceased to exist.

XIII

Three years before Carthage was demolished, Marcus Cato, who had been a constant advocate for its destruction, died, in the consulship of Lucius Censorinus and Marcus Manlius. In the very year in which Carthage fell, Lucius Mummius utterly destroyed Corinth, nine hundred and fifty-two years after it had been built by Aletes the son of Hippotes. Each of the generals was honoured with a name from the people whom he conquered, the one being styled Africanus, the other Achaicus. No new man[22], before Mummius, had ever assumed a surname derived from military merit. Of these two commanders, the dispositions, as well as the pursuits, were entirely different. Scipio was so elegant a cultivator and admirer of liberal studies, and of every kind of learning, that he had constantly with him, at home and in the field, two men of eminent talents, Polybius and Panætius; for no man balanced the fatigues of business with the enjoyments of leisure more judiciously than Scipio, as he was constantly studying the arts either of war or of peace, and constantly exercising either his body in toil or his mind in learning. Mummius, on the contrary, was so extremely ignorant, that when, on the taking of Corinth, he was hiring persons to carry pictures and statues, finished by the hands of the greatest masters, into Italy, he ordered notice to be given to the contractors, that, if they lost any of them, they must find new ones. Yet I think you, Vinicius, must be of opinion, that it would have been more for the advantage of our countrymen that their minds should have remained still ignorant of Corinthian elegancies, than that their knowledge of them should have reached its present height; and that the ancient ignorance would have been more conducive to the public honour than our modern skill.

XIV

As a view of any historical subject, when contracted into one continuous narrative, is retained more easily in the eye and the memory than when left dispersed in different periods, I have determined to introduce between the former and latter part of this volume, a summary of particulars on a not unimportant subject, and to specify, in this part of my work, what colonies, since the capture of Rome by the Gauls, have been established by order of the senate, and at what times; for of the military settlements the occasions and founders are sufficiently known from their names. With this detail I shall unite, I think without impropriety, an account of the enlargement of the state, and the extension of the Roman name, by the communication of its privileges.

Seven years after the Gauls took the city, the colony of Sutrium was settled; the year after, that of Setia; and, after an interval of nine years, that of Nepe. Two-and-thirty years afterwards, the Aricians received the civic franchise. Three hundred and sixty-two years ago, in the consulship of Spurius Posthumius and Veturius Calvinus, the freedom of the city, but without the right of voting, was given to the Campanians and part of the Samnites; and the same year a colony was settled at Cales. Three years afterwards, the people of Fundi and Formiæ were admitted as citizens, in the very year that Alexandria was founded. In the following consulship, when Spurius Posthumius and Philo Publilius were censors, the civic franchise was granted to Acerra. Three years afterwards, that of Luceria; in four years more, that of Suessa Aurunca, and two years later, those of Saticula and Interamna. Then followed ten years in which nothing of the kind occurred; at the end of which time were established the colonies of Sora and Alba, and two years afterwards that of Carseoli. In the consulate of Quintus Fabius for the fifth time, and that of Decius Mus for the fourth time, the year in which Pyrrhus began to reign, colonies were sent to Sinuessa and Minturnæ, and four years afterwards to Venusia. After an interval of two years, in the consulate of Marcus Curius and Rufinus

Cornelius, the rights of citizenship, but without that of voting, were given to the Sabines; an event which took place about three hundred and twenty years ago. About three hundred years ago, in the consulship of Fabius Dorso and Claudius Canina, colonies were sent to Cosa and Pæstum, and five years afterwards, in the consulship of Sempronius Sophus and Appius, the son of Appius Cæcus, to Ariminum and Beneventum; and the right of voting was then granted to the Sabines. At the commencement of the first Punic war, Firmum and Castrum were occupied with colonies, and the following year Æsernia; in seventeen years afterwards Æsulum and Alsium; two years later, Fregenæ; in the next year, when Torquatus and Sempronius were consuls, Brundisium; three years after, in the year when the games of Flora commenced, Spoletium. Two years later, Valentia was colonised, and, about the time of Hannibal's arrival in Italy, Cremona and Placentia.

XV

Neither while Hannibal remained in Italy, nor for several years immediately succeeding his departure, had the Romans any opportunities of founding colonies; for, while the war lasted, they were obliged to press soldiers, instead of discharging them, and, when it was ended, their strength required to be recruited rather than dispersed. However, in the consulship of Manlius Volso and Fabius Nobilior, about two hundred and seventeen years ago, the colony of Bononia was settled, and five years afterwards, those of Pisaurum and Potentia; in three years more, Aquileia and Gravisca; four years later, Luca. During the same period, though some express a doubt of it, colonies were sent to Puteoli, Salernum, and Buxentum. One hundred and eighty-seven years ago, a colony was sent to Auximum in the Picenian territory; this took place three years before Cassius the censor began to build the theatre looking from the Lupercal[23] towards Mount Palatine, when the great austerity of manners, and the consul Scipio, prevented him[24] from completing it; an occurrence which I number among the most honourable testimonies to the public character in those days. In the consulship of Cassius Longinus and Sextius Calvinus, (who defeated the Salyes[25] at the springs which were from him named Aquæ Sextiae,) about one hundred and fifty-seven years ago, the colony of Fabrateria was settled, and the year after those of Scylacium, Minervium, Tarentum, and Neptunia, as well as Carthage in Africa[26], which was, I have said, the first colony planted beyond the bounds of Italy. Concerning Dertona there is no certainty; but Narbo Martius in Gaul was settled in the consulship of Porcius and Marcius, about a hundred and fifty-three years ago. Twenty-three years after was founded Eporedia among the Bagienni[27], when Marius was consul, for the sixth time, with Valerius Flaccus. Any colony settled since that time, except the military colonies, I am unable to recollect.

XVI

Though this little portion of my work has exceeded the limits intended, and though I am sensible that in so hasty a composition, which, like a wheel or rapid torrent[28], allows me nowhere to make a stand, I ought rather to omit some things that may seem necessary than to introduce any that are superfluous, I yet cannot refrain from noticing a point on which I have often reflected, and on which I could never arrive at any satisfactory conclusion. For who can sufficiently wonder, that the most eminent geniuses in every art have agreed in one common character, and have fallen within one period of time; and that, as different kinds of animals, shut up in a fold or other inclosure, continue each distinct from those around it, and form themselves into separate bodies, so minds, capable of any great achievements, have formed distinct assemblages about the same time and with similar effect? One age, and that not extending through many years, gave lustre to tragedy by the works of those great authors, men animated by a divine spirit, Æschylus, Sophocles, and Euripides. One age produced the Ancient Comedy, under Cratinus, Aristophanes, and Eupolis. As for the New Comedy, Menander, with Philemon and Diphilus, his equals in age rather than ability, not only invented it within a few years, but left works in it beyond imitation. The distinguished philosophers, too, deriving their knowledge from the lips of Socrates, in how short a time did they all, whom I have a little before enumerated[29], flourish after the death of Plato and Aristotle! And in oratory what splendour was there before Isocrates, or after the death of his hearers and their immediate disciples? So crowded were they into a short space of time, that all who were worthy of being remembered must have been known to each other.

XVII

Nor has this peculiarity occurred more among the Greeks than among the Romans. Roman tragedy, unless we go back to the rudest and most barbarous efforts, which deserve no praise but as attempts at invention, subsists wholly in the writings of Accius and his contemporaries. The agreeable sportiveness of Latin humour displayed itself, about the same time, in Cæcilius, Terence, and Afranius[30]. As for the historians, a period of less than eighty years (even if we include Livy in the age of the earlier writers) produced them all, with the exception of Cato and some old and obscure annalists. Nor did the assemblage of poets extend further in time, either upwards or downwards. With respect to oratory, forensic pleading, and the perfect beauty of prose eloquence, they burst forth complete (to say nothing of Cato, and to speak with due respect for Publius Crassus, Scipio, Lælius, the Gracchi, Fannius, and Servius Galba) under Cicero, who was the coryphæus in his art; as of all other orators we receive pleasure from few, and admire none, except such as lived in his time, or immediately succeeded it[31]. That the same has been the case with regard to grammarians, statuaries, painters, and sculptors[32], whoever investigates the records of ages will easily convince himself, and will see that the most eminent performances in every art are confined within very narrow limits of time.

Of this concurrence of similar geniuses in the same period, of their corresponding devotion to like pursuits, and their equality of progress, I often inquire for the causes, but find none that I can regard as satisfactory. Some, however, I discover that are probable; among which are the following. Emulation nourishes genius; and at one time envy, at another admiration, kindles a spirit of imitation. Any art, too, which is pursued with extreme zeal, will soon reach the height of excellence; and to stand still on the summit is difficult; as, in the natural course of things, what cannot advance, recedes. And as we are at first excited with ardour to overtake those whom we think our superiors, so, when we once despair of surpassing or equalling them, our zeal flags with our hope, ceases to pursue what it cannot attain, and, relinquishing that object as already pre-occupied, turns to something new. Declining any pursuit in which we cannot arrive at eminence, we endeavour to find one that will allow scope for our exertions; and the consequence is, that such changes, if frequent and unsteady, prove the greatest obstacle to perfection.

XVIII

Our wonder may well be transferred from ages to cities. One city in Attica was distinguished in eloquence for a greater number of years, and for more achievements in it, than all the rest of Greece; so that, though the natives of that country were dispersed through its different states, we might suppose its genius to have been confined entirely within the walls of Athens. Nor do I more wonder that this should have been the case, than that not a single orator of Argos, Thebes, or Lacedæmon, was thought worthy of notice during his life, or of remembrance after his death. In such studies, these, as well as many other cities, were wholly unproductive, except that the single muse of Pindar conferred some degree of lustre on Thebes. Alcman[33] the Lacedæmonians falsely claim. * * * *

References

1 I. [Epeus,] being parted, &c.] The name is wanting in the text at the commencement of this fragment. But it appears from Justin, xx., 2, as well as from Aristotle, De Miraculis, that it was Epeus, the builder of the Trojan horse, (doli fabricator Epeus, Virg. Æn., ii., 264,) who founded Metapontum.

2 Metapontum] On the coast of Lucania, in the south of Italy.

3 His brother] Ajax, who was refused the arms of Achilles.

4 Phidippus] An inferior leader in the Trojan war, from the isles of Calydnæ, on the coast of Caria. Hom. Il., ii., 678.

5 His cousin] Patruelis. He was son of Thyestes, brother of Atreus, Agamemnon's father.

6 Tyrrhenus] He gave name, it is said, to Tyrrhenia, Tuscia, or Etruria, in Italy. The story of his departure from Lydia is taken from Herod., i., 94.

7 Without being known] Imprudenter. "He was slain by the enemy, not being aware that he was the king." Lipsius.

8 III. Thessalus, the son of Hercules] Father of Phidippus above mentioned. Homer, loc. cit.

9 Rebuilt] Condidit. "Ex integro restituit." Vossius.

10 V. An exclusive right, &c.] Solus appellari poeta meruit. "Non summus modo; splendidum judicium." Krause.

11 VI. System of education most suitable] Disciplinæ convenientissimæ [vir]. I have omitted vir, which, as Ruhnken says, "nullo pacto tolerari potest." Heinsius would alter it to virtuti; Ruhnken to viribus; and some other critics, as Krause signifies, having proposed viris.

12 At the end of this chapter is inserted, in all the editions, a passage from Æmilius (or rather, as Krause thinks, Manilius) Sura. Some person, in old times, seems to have written it in the margin of his manuscript, whence it crept into the text. I have omitted it.

13 VIII. Feast of Pales] April 21st.

14 Patricians] Patricii, from patres. Comp. Flor., i., 1.

15 IX. Proved a more powerful enemy] Here is a great hiatus, all the history of Rome being lost from the foundation of the city to the year U.C. 582. The commencement of the chapter stands thus: . . . . quam timuerit hostis, expetit. Lipsius, for expetit, would substitute extitit, and thinks that the author had written something to this effect: Populo Romano gravior, quam timuerat, hostis extitit, nempe Perses. See Florus, ii., 12.

16 His brother's] Attalus.

17 Two hundred thousand sestertia] 1,776,041l. 13s. 4d.

18 X. Partner with him in property] Consors. "Consortes are properly coheirs, inheriting a property in common, which they suffer to remain, at least for a time, undivided." Burman.

19 XI. Private custody] Liberâ custodiâ. See Sall., Cat., c. 47.

20 The Achæans] Achæos. That is, the Greeks. The Romans called Greece, as their province, Achaia. See Florus, ii., 7.

21 A temple of marble] Ædem ex marmore. Burman would take ædem for ædes, understanding a private house for Metellus himself; but this, as Krause says, is not only invitâ Latinitate, but invitâ historiâ; for marble was not used in the erection of private houses till a much later period.

22 XIII. New man] See Sall., Cat., c. 23.

23 XV. From the Lupercal] A Lupercali. "The Lupercal was a grotto sacred to Pan, near the Palatine mount." Krause.

24 When the great austerity of manners—prevented him, &c.] There are various readings of this passage, but all producing much the same sense. Krause reads, Cui (Cassio) id demoliendo—restitêre; that is, "the austerity of manners, and Scipio the consul, opposed Cassius by pulling it (the theatre) down."

25 Salyes] A people of Gallia Narbonensis.

26 Carthage in Africa] A colony was established on the site of the old city by the Gracchi, and called Colonia Carthago.

27 Bagienni] Otherwise called Vagienni, a people of Liguria, near the source of the Po.

28 XVI. Torrent] Gurgitis. The words ac verticis, which follow this, and which Ruhnken and Krause think a mere gloss, I have omitted.

29 Whom I have a little before enumerated] Quos paulo ante enumeravimus. In some part of the book which is now lost.

30 Cæcilius, Terence, and Afranius] Why does he omit Plautus? "I must suppose either that the name of Plautus has dropped out of the text, or, what seems more probable, that Paterculus entertained the same opinion of Plautus as Horace expresses, De Arte Poeticâ, 270, and therefore intentionally omitted him." Krause.

31 Except such as lived in his time, or immediately succeeded it] Neminem—nisi aut ab illo visum, aut qui illum viderit. This is translated according to the interpretation of Krause. Those who were visi ab illo were his contemporaries, (some of them, perhaps, a little his seniors,) with whom he lived, as it were, face to face; those qui illum viderunt were the men of the succeeding generation, who were just old enough to have had a sight of him. Thus Ovid says of Virgil, Virgilium tantum vidi.

32 Statuaries—sculptors] Plastis—scalptoribus. Plastes, one that makes figures of any soft matter, as clay; scalptor, or sculptor, one who works with harder material, as stone or wood.

33 XVIII. Alcman] He was a native of Lydia, and brought to Lacedæmon when very young, as a slave.

BOOK II

I

The former Scipio had opened for the Romans the way to power; the latter[1] opened that to luxury. For when their dread of Carthage was at an end, and their rival in empire was removed, the nation, deserting the cause of virtue, went over, not gradually, but with precipitation, to that of vice; the old rules of conduct were renounced, and new introduced; and the people turned themselves from activity to slumber, from arms to pleasure, from business to idleness. Then it was that Scipio built porticos on the Capitol; that Metellus erected those before mentioned[2]; and that Cnæus Octavius raised that pre-eminently delightful one in the Circus; and private luxury soon followed public magnificence.

There soon succeeded a lamentable and disgraceful war in Spain, conducted by Viriathus, a captain of banditti; which, though it proceeded with various changes of fortune, was oftener adverse than favourable to the Romans. And Viriathus, rather through the treachery than valour of Servilius Cæpio, being killed, a still more violent war with Numantia burst forth. This city never had under arms more than ten thousand of its inhabitants, yet, whether from the obstinacy of their spirit, the inexperience of our generals, or the caprice of fortune, it compelled both Pompeius, a man of great reputation, (the first of the name who held the consulship,) to sign a treaty of peace on most dishonourable terms, and the consul Mancinus Hostilius to make another not less mean and disgraceful. Interest secured Pompey from punishment; but the modesty of Mancinus, by shrinking from no penalty[3], led to his being surrendered by heralds to the enemy, stripped of his robes, and with his hands tied behind his back. But the Numantines, acting like the people of Caudium in former times, refused to receive him, saying that a public violation of faith was not to be expiated by the blood of an individual.

II

This surrender of Mancinus excited violent dissensions in the state. For Tiberius Gracchus, (son of a most illustrious and eminent citizen, and grandson, on his mother's side, of Publius Africanus,) who had been quæstor at the time, and by whose encouragement that treaty had been concluded, was both grievously offended at the annulling of it, and entertained apprehensions for himself of a similar sentence or punishment; from which causes, though in his other conduct a man of the strictest integrity, endowed with the highest abilities, and pure and upright in his intentions, in short, adorned with every virtue of which man when perfected both by nature and cultivation is susceptible, he, on being appointed tribune of the people in the consulate of Publius Mutius Scævola and Lucius Calpurnius, a hundred and sixty-two years ago, deserted the worthy party, and by promising the rights of citizens to all the inhabitants of Italy, and proposing at the same time agrarian laws, threw all things, while all men were eager to secure a footing in the state[4], into the utmost confusion, and brought the Commonwealth into imminent danger, of which it was for some time doubtful what would be the event. Octavius, one of his colleagues, who stood up in defence of the public good, he compelled to resign his office, and procured the election of himself, his father-in-law Appius, who had been consul, and his brother Gracchus, then very young, as commissioners to distribute lands, and settle colonies.

III

On this, Publius Scipio Nasica, grandson of him who had been pronounced by the senate the best man in the state, son of him who in his censorship had built the porticos to the Capitol, and great grandson of Cnæus Scipio, a man of very illustrious character, uncle of Publius Africanus; this Scipio, I say, though not invested with any military or public office, and though he was cousin to Tiberius Gracchus, yet, preferring his country to family connexion, and considering whatever injured the public as hurtful to each individual, (for which merits he was afterwards, in his absence, created chief pontiff; the first instance of the kind,) wrapped the lappet of his gown round his left arm, and mounted to the upper part of the Capitol; where, standing on the summit of the steps, he called on all that desired the safety of the Commonwealth to follow him. Immediately the chief of the nobility, the senate, the greater and better part of the equestrian body, and such plebeians as were unallured by the pernicious views of the Gracchi, rushed together against Gracchus, who, with some bands of his partisans, was standing in the court, haranguing a concourse of people from almost every part of Italy. Betaking himself to flight, he was struck, as he was running down the descent from the Capitol, with a piece of a broken bench, and thus prematurely closed a life which he might have passed with the greatest honour. This was the commencement of civil bloodshed, and of impunity to the sword, in Rome. Henceforward right was oppressed by strength; the more powerful were the more highly esteemed; disputes between citizens, which were formerly settled on amicable terms, were decided by the sword; and wars were undertaken, not for honourable reasons, but from prospects of gain. Nor can this excite our wonder; for examples do not stop where they begin; but, if allowed to spread through a channel ever so narrow, make way for themselves to any extent; and, when men have once deviated from the right path, they are hurried headlong into wrong; and no one thinks that dishonourable to himself which is gainful to another.

IV

During the course of these transactions in Italy, Aristonicus, who, on the death of king Attalus, by whom Asia had been bequeathed to the people of Rome, (as Bithynia was afterwards bequeathed to them by Nicomedes,) pretending to be sprung from the royal family, had seized the government by force of arms, was conquered, and led in triumph by Marcus Perperna, and afterwards put to death by Manius Aquilius, for having, at the commencement of hostilities, killed the proconsul Crassus Mucianus, a man eminent for his knowledge of the law, as he was on his journey out of the country.

After so many defeats experienced at Numantia, Publius Scipio Africanus Æmilianus, the destroyer of Carthage, being elected a second time consul, and sent into Spain, supported in that country the character for conduct and success that he had acquired in Africa, and within a year and three months after his arrival levelled Numantia, after surrounding and shaking it with batteries, to the ground. Nor did any man of any nation, before his time, consecrate his name to perpetual remembrance by a more remarkable destruction of cities; for, by the overthrow of Carthage and Numantia, he freed us from the dread of the one, and from the dishonour that we suffered from the other. It was this Scipio, who, being asked by Carbo, a tribune, what he thought of the killing of Tiberius Gracchus, replied, that if he had any thought of usurping the government, he was justly slain; and, when the whole assembly cried out against him, he exclaimed, "After having so often heard, without fear, the shouts of armed enemies, how can I be alarmed at the cries of such as you, to whom Italy is but a stepmother[5]?" Returning, from a short absence, into the city, in the consulate of Manius Aquilius and Caius Sempronius, a hundred and fifty-eight years ago, after his two consulships and two triumphs, and after having removed two objects of terror to his country, he was found one morning dead in his bed, and marks of strangulation were observed on his neck. Yet concerning the death of great a man no inquiry was made; and the body of him by whose services Rome had raised her head above the world, was carried to its burial-place with the head veiled[6]. Whether he died a natural death, as most people think, or came to his end, as some have asserted, by treachery, he certainly passed a life of such honour that it is eclipsed by none before his time except that of his grandfather. He died at about fifty-four years of age. If any one questions this, let him look back to Scipio's first consulship, to which he was elected at the age of thirty-six, and doubt no more.

V

Before the destruction of Numantia, the military efforts of Decimus Brutus in Spain had been remarkable; so that, having made his way though all the nations of that country, subdued vast multitudes of men, and a great number of cities, and visited places of which the names had scarcely been heard, he merited the surname of Gallæcus. A few years before him, military obedience, under Quintus Macedonicus, was enforced in that country with such severity that, while he was besieging a city named Contrebia, he ordered five legionary cohorts, which had been repulsed in an attack on a very steep place, to mount it again immediately. Though all the soldiers made their wills in preparation for action, as if going to certain destruction, the obstinate general was not deterred from his purpose, and saw his men return with victory, whom he had sent out in expectation of death. So great was the effect of shame blended with fear, and of hope springing from despair. He gained much credit for courage and strictness; but Fabius Æmilianus showed in Spain the most noble example of discipline.

VI

After an interval of ten years, the same rage which had animated Tiberius Gracchus, seized his brother Caius, who, resembling him in all his virtues as well as in his want of judgment, was in abilities and eloquence far his superior; and who, though he might, without the least anxiety of mind, have become the very first man in the state, yet, prompted by a desire either of revenging his brother's death, or of preparing a way for himself to regal power, he entered on a tribuneship of similar character to that of his brother, forming projects, however, much more extensive and influential. He designed to extend the civic franchise to all the Italians, as far almost as the Alps; to divide the lands, and to prohibit every citizen from possessing more than five hundred acres; a restriction which had once been enjoined by the Licinian law. He likewise wished to lay new taxes on imported goods, to fill the provinces with new colonies, to transfer the privilege of being judges[7] from the senators to the knights, and to distribute corn to the populace; in short, he was resolved to leave nothing quiet and undisturbed, nothing in the condition in which he found it. He even procured himself to be re-elected tribune. But the consul Lucius Opimius, who in his prætorship had demolished Fregellæ, attacked him with an armed force, and put him to death, and together with him Fulvius Flaccus, a man who had been consul, and had triumphed, but was equally inclined to noxious measures; and whom Gaius Gracchus had nominated a commissioner in the room of his brother Tiberius, and associated with himself to be a sharer in his king-like power. One particular in Opimius's conduct is mentioned deserving of reprobation, namely, that he offered a reward for the head, not merely of Gracchus, but of any turbulent Roman citizen, promising its weight in gold. Flaccus, while he was collecting a party in arms on the Aventine, with intent to make resistance, was killed, together with his elder son; Gracchus, attempting to escape, and being nearly overtaken by a party sent by Opimius, held out his neck to Euporus his slave, who slew himself with the same fortitude with which he relieved his master.

Pomponius, a Roman knight, showed on that day a singular degree of attachment to Gracchus; for, like Cocles, he withstood his enemies on the bridge, and then run himself through with his sword. The body of Caius Gracchus, with great barbarity on the part of the victors, was thrown into the Tiber, as had previously been the case with that of Tiberius.

VII

Such was the latter part of the lives, and such the deaths, of the sons of Tiberius Gracchus, the grandsons of Publius Scipio Africanus, men who made a bad use of the best talents, and who died while their mother, the daughter of Africanus, was still alive. Had these men fixed their desires on any degree of eminence compatible with civil liberty, (whatever it was that they sought to gain by their turbulent proceedings,) the public would have granted it without an effort on their part. To the severity before mentioned, was added an act of unparalleled barbarity. A youth of uncommon beauty, in the eighteenth year of his age, son of Fulvius Flaccus, but innocent of his father's offences, being sent to negotiate terms of accommodation, was ordered to be put to death by Opimius. A Tuscan soothsayer, his friend, seeing the lad weep as he was dragged to prison, said to him, "Why do you not rather act thus?" And immediately dashing his head against a stone pillar at the prison-door, beat out his brains, and expired.

Examinations of the friends and clients of the Gracchi were soon after held, and with great severity. Hence, when Opimius, who, in other matters was upright and respected, was afterwards condemned on a trial before the people, no commiseration was shown him by his countrymen, through their recollection of his former want of feeling. The same general odium afterwards deservedly crushed, under trials before the people, Rutilius and Popillius, who, being consuls at the time, had acted cruelly towards the friends of Tiberius Gracchus. Amongst affairs of such importance I shall mention one of which the knowledge is of little consequence. This is the Opimius, from whom, when he was consul, the celebrated Opimian wine was named. That there is none of it at present may be inferred from the distance of time, for between his consulate and yours, Marcus Vinicius, a hundred and fifty-one years have elapsed. The conduct of Opimius met the less approbation, because his object was revenge from personal enmity; and his severity seemed to have been inflicted to satisfy, not public justice, but private hatred.

VIII

[Soon after, in the consulate of Marcius and Porcius, the colony of Narbo Marcius was settled[8].] Let the strictness of judicial proceedings in those times be here recorded. Caius Cato, who had been consul, and who was grandson of Marcus Cato, and son of the sister of Africanus, was convicted of extortion committed in Macedonia, and fined eighteen sestertia[9]; for judges then considered the inclination of the man to dishonesty rather than the magnitude of the offence, and estimated deeds, in general, by intention, regarding rather what had been done than to how great an extent. About the same time, the two Metelli, brothers, triumphed on one day. Another instance of distinction not less honourable, and hitherto unparalleled, was, that the two sons of Fulvius Flaccus, him who had taken Capua, were joined together in the consulship. One of them indeed had been adopted, and received into the family of Manlius Acidinus. As to the two Metelli, who were censors together, they were cousins-german, not brothers; the circumstance of two full brothers being united in office fell to the lot of none but the Scipios[10]. At this time the Cimbri and Teutones came across the Rhine, and soon made themselves notorious by the calamities that they brought on us and on themselves. At the same time, there was celebrated a brilliant triumph of Minucius, him who built the porticos now so much admired, over the Scordisci.

IX

During this period flourished those eminent orators Scipio Æmilianus, Lælius, Servius Galba, the two Gracchi, Caius Fannius, Papirius Carbo, and, above all, Lucius Crassus and Marcus Antonius. Nor must we omit Metellus Numidicus, or Scaurus. These, in time as well as genius, were followed by Caius Cæsar Strabo and Publius Sulpicius. As to Quintus Mucius, he was more noted for his knowledge of the law than for eloquence. During the same age appeared the bright genius of Afranius in comedy, and those of Pacuvius and Attius in tragedy; geniuses who rise into competition with the spirit of the Greeks. Then were displayed, too, the powers of Ennius[11], who claims for his works an honourable place with theirs; for, though they wrote with more correctness, he seems to have had the greater share of energy. A distinguished name was likewise acquired by Lucilius, who in the Numantine war had served in the cavalry under Publius Africanus. At the same time Jugurtha and Marius, then both young, learned in the same camp under Africanus that skill which they were afterwards to practise in opposite camps. Sisenna the historian was then young, but some years after, at a more advanced age, published his history of the civil wars, and those of Sylla. Cœlius was prior to Sisenna: coeval with him were Rutilius, Claudius Quadrigarius, and Valerius Antias. We must not, however, forget that Pomponius lived in this age, a writer admired for his thoughts, though rude in language, and chiefly deserving notice for the novelty of what he invented[12].

X

Let us here record a severe act of the censors Cassius Longinus and Cæpio, who, a hundred and fifty-five years ago, summoned before them an augur, Æmilius Lepidus, because he rented a house at six sestertia[13]. At present, if any person lived at so low a rent, he would scarcely be acknowledged as a senator: so soon do people proceed from the reasonable to the unreasonable, from the unreasonable to the vicious, from the vicious to the extravagant. During this period a remarkable victory was gained by Domitius over the Arverni, and another by Fabius over the Allobroges. Fabius, who was grandson of Paulus, acquired from his success the surname of Allobrogicus. Here we may observe a peculiar kind of happiness attending the Domitian family, which was highly distinguished, though confined to a small number. Before the present Cnæus Domitius, a youth of most remarkable goodness of disposition, there were seven of that family, the only sons of their respective parents, who all arrived at a consulship and priesthood, and almost all at the honours of a triumph.

XI

The Jugurthine war was then conducted by Quintus Metellus, a commander inferior to no one of the age. Under him acted, as lieutenant-general, Caius Marius, whom we mentioned above, a man of mean birth, coarse and rough in his manners, but of strict temperance[14], who, in proportion as he was excellent in war, was fatal to peace. He was immoderately eager for glory, his ambition was insatiable, his passions ungovernable, so that he was never at rest. By disseminating, through farmers of the revenue, and others who traded in Africa, insinuations against Metellus, as being dilatory in his operations, and purposely protracting the war to the third year, as well as invectives against the natural pride of the nobles, and their ambition to continue in posts of power, he succeeded, after obtaining leave of absence to come to Rome, in procuring his election to the consulship, and getting the management of the war, now nearly terminated by Metellus, who had twice routed Jugurtha in the field, intrusted to himself. Nevertheless, the triumph of Metellus was exceedingly magnificent, and the surname of Numidicus, which he had well earned by his merits in the field, was conferred upon him. As we previously noticed the splendid fortune of the Domitian family, we may here mention that of the Cæcilian, for within about twelve years of this time there were above twelve Metelli either consuls or censors, or who enjoyed triumphs. Hence it would appear that the fortune of families, like that of cities and empires, flourishes, fades, and decays.

XII

Caius Marius, at this early time, had Lucius Sylla connected with him in quality of quæstor, as if from some precaution of the fates[15], and having sent him ambassador to king Bocchus, received, through his means, king Jugurtha as a prisoner; an event which took place a hundred and thirty-eight years ago. Being elected consul a second time, and returning to Rome, he led Jugurtha in triumph on the first of January, the day on which his second consulship commenced. As the overwhelming force of the German tribes, the Cimbri and Teutones mentioned above, had vanquished and put to flight in Gaul the consuls Cæpio and Manlius, as well as Carbo and Silanus previously, and had dispersed their armies, and killed Aurelius Scaurus the consul, as well as other leaders of great reputation, the Roman people deemed that no commander was better qualified than Marius to repel such formidable enemies. Thenceforward consulships multiplied on him. His third was spent in preparations for the war, and in the same year Cnæus Domitius, a tribune of the people, got a law passed, that the people should appoint priests, who were formerly elected by the sacerdotal body. In his fourth he engaged the Teutones, at Aquæ Sextiæ, beyond the Alps, and in two successive days slew a hundred and fifty thousand of them, and utterly reduced their nation. In his fifth, he himself, and the proconsul Quintus Lutatius Catulus, met the Cimbri on what are called the Raudian plains, on this side of the Alps, and put an end to the war by a most successful battle, killing or taking above a hundred thousand men. By these victories Marius seems to have deserved that his country should not regret his birth; and to have made amends by his services for the evils that he brought upon it. The sixth was conferred on him as a reward for his merits. Yet must not this consulship be defrauded of its due share of praise, for, during the course of it, the consul repressed, with an armed force, the excesses of Servilius, Glaucia, and Saturninus Apuleius, who, maintaining themselves in office, were inflicting deep wounds on the constitution, and dispersing the assemblies of the people with violence and bloodshed; and he at last put those pestilent disturbers to death in the Curia Hostilia[16].

XIII

At the end of a few succeeding years, Marcus Livius Drusus entered on the office of tribune; a man of the noblest birth, the greatest eloquence, and the strictest purity of life; but who, in all his undertakings, was more distinguished by ability and good intention than by success. He formed a design of restoring to the senate its ancient dignity, and of transferring from the knights to that body the right of being judges; because when the knights, by the Sempronian laws, were invested with that authority, they had treated with cruel severity many of the most illustrious and most innocent citizens; and in particular had brought to trial for extortion Publius Rutilius, a man distinguished for virtue not only above his own, but above any age, and, to the exceeding great grief of the public, had condemned him to pay a penalty. But in those very efforts which he made in favour of the senate, he found the senate itself opposed to him. For they did not perceive that whatever he brought forward in favour of the plebeians was intended to allure and attract the multitude, in order that, being gratified in smaller matters, they might consent to others of greater importance. Such, indeed, was the fate of Drusus, that the senate favoured the injurious proceedings of his colleagues more than his own excellent designs, rejecting with scorn the honour offered by him, while they submitted patiently to the wrong done them by the others; looking, in short, with envy on his very exalted reputation, and with indulgence on the mean characters of his opponents.

XIV

When such well-intended plans were badly received, the purpose of Drusus was changed, and he resolved to extend the civic franchise to all Italy. As he was taking measures for this purpose, on coming home one day from the forum, surrounded by the immense, disorderly crowd that constantly attended him, he was stabbed in the court-yard of his own house with a knife, which was left sticking in his side, and within a few hours expired. While he was drawing almost his last breath, he uttered an expression, as he looked on the crowd standing round and lamenting over him, very consonant to his inward feelings. "My relations and friends," said he, "will the Commonwealth ever again have a citizen like me?" Thus ended the life of this illustrious man. One incident which marks the goodness of his disposition must not be omitted. When he was building a house on the Palatine Mount, on the spot where that stands which formerly was Cicero's, afterwards Censorinus's, and now belongs to Statilius Sisenna, and the architect offered to construct it in such a manner, than it would be proof against all overlookers, no one being able even to cast a glance into it, "Rather," replied he, "if you have such skill, construct my house in such a manner, that whatever I do may be seen by all."

XV

[Among the most pernicious measures introduced by the laws of Gracchus, I reckon the planting of colonies out of Italy. Such a proceeding our ancestors had so carefully avoided, (because they saw Carthage so much more powerful than its mother city Tyre; Marseilles than Phocæa; Syracuse than Corinth; Cyzicus and Byzantium than Miletus,) that they even called home Roman citizens from the provinces to be registered by the censors in Italy. The first colony planted beyond the limits of Italy was Carthage[17].] The death of Drusus hastened the breaking out of the Italian war, which had been gathering to a head during a considerable time before; for in the consulate of Lucius Cæsar and Publius Rutilius, a hundred and twenty years from the present, all Italy took arms against the Romans. This unfortunate insurrection had its origin among the people of Asculum, (who killed Servius a prætor, and Fonteius a lieutenant-general,) and from them it soon spread to the Marsians, and diffused itself through every quarter of the country. As the subsequent sufferings of those people were very severe, so were their demands extremely just; for they claimed the privileges of a country, whose power they supported by their arms; every year, and for every war, they furnished a double number of men, both horse and foot, and yet were not admitted to the privileges of the state, which, by their services, had arrived at that very eminence from which it looked down with disdain on men of the same nation and blood, as aliens and foreigners. This war carried off above three hundred thousand of the flower of Italy. The Roman generals most distinguished in it were, Cnæus Pompey, father of Cnæus Pompey the Great; Caius Marius before mentioned; Lucius Sylla, who was prætor in the preceding year; and Quintus Metellus, son of Numidicus, who deservedly obtained the surname of Pius: for when his father was banished by Lucius Saturninus, a tribune of the people, because he alone refused to swear obedience to his laws, the son, by his

19

dutiful exertions, and with the sanction of the senate, and the approbation of the Roman people, procured his recal. So that Numidicus was not more honoured by his triumphs and distinctions than by the cause of his exile, the exile itself, and his return from it.

XVI

The most remarkable leaders of the Italians were Silo Popædius, Herius Asinius, Insteius Cato, Caius Pontidius, Telesinus Pontius, Marius Egnatius, and Papius Mutilus. Nor shall I, through mistaken modesty, withhold any part of the praise due to my own family, while I relate only the truth; for much honour ought to be paid to the memory of Minatius Magius of Æculanum, my ancestor in the fourth degree. He was grandson of Decius Magius, (a man of high distinction and trust among the Campanians,) and displayed in this war such a faithful attachment to the Romans, that, when a legion which he himself had raised among the Hirpinians, he, in conjunction with Titus Didius, took Herculaneum, and with Lucius Sylla besieged Pompeii, and gained possession of Compsa. His virtues have been celebrated by several writers, but by Hortensius, in his Annals, more fully and clearly than by any other. The Roman people amply recompensed his fidelity, by voting him a citizen with peculiar distinction, and electing his two sons prætors, at a time when only six were elected. So variable and alarming was the fortune of the Italian war, that in the course of two successive years two Roman consuls, first Rutilius and afterwards Porcius Cato, were slain by the enemy, and the armies of the Roman people discomfited in several places, so that a general assumption of the military dress[18] took place, and was long continued. The enemy chose for their seat of government the city of Corfinium, which they renamed Italicum. The strength of the Romans was afterwards recruited, though slowly, by admitting into citizenship such as either had not taken arms, or had laid them down early, while the exertions of Pompey, Sylla, and Marius, revived the energy of the government when it was debilitated and ready to sink.

XVII

An end being now nearly put, except where the remains of hostility continued at Nola, to the Italian war, (the result of which was that the Romans, themselves exhausted, consented to grant the privilege of citizenship to certain state that were vanquished and reduced, rather than to the whole when flourishing in unimpaired strength,) Quintus Pompeius and Lucius Cornelius Sylla entered upon their consulship. Sylla was a man, who, before he had subdued his competitors, could not be sufficiently commended, nor afterwards too severely censured. He was of a noble family, being the sixth in descent from Cornelius Rufinus, one of the most celebrated leaders in the war with Pyrrhus; but as the lustre of the family had been for some time obscured, he conducted himself, through a great part of his life, in such a manner, that he seemed to have no thought of standing for the consulship. However, after his prætorship, having acquired great reputation in the Italian war, (such as he had before gained when lieutenant-general under Marius in Gaul, where he defeated some of the enemy's most eminent commanders,) he assumed courage from success, and becoming a candidate for the consulship, was elected by the almost universal suffrage of his countrymen. When he attained this honour, he was in the forty-ninth year of his age.

XVIII

About this time Mithridates king of Pontus, a prince who must neither be passed without notice, nor be slightly mentioned; a man most active in war, pre-eminent in courage, distinguished sometimes by success and always by spirit; in council a general, in action a soldier, and in hatred to the Romans another Hannibal, took forcible possession of Asia, and put to death all the Roman citizens that were in it, whom, by sending letters to the different states, filled with promises of great rewards, he procured to be slain on the same day and hour. At this crisis no people equalled the Rhodians, either in resolute exertions against Mithridates, or in firm attachment to the Romans; and a lustre was thrown on their fidelity by the perfidy of the Mitylenæans, who gave up in chains to Mithridates, Manius Aquillius and several others; and yet to these very Mitylenæans liberty was afterwards granted by Pompey, merely to gratify Theophanes[19]. Mithridates, now becoming formidable, seemed to threaten even Italy, when the province of Asia fell to the lot of Sylla. After leaving Rome, he stayed some time in the neighbourhood of Nola; (for that city, as if repenting of the fidelity to us, which it had sacredly maintained during the Punic war, continued in arms with persevering obstinacy, and was then besieged by a Roman army;) during which interval, Publius Sulpicius, a tribune of the people, an eloquent and active man, distinguished for wealth, interest, the number of his friends, and the vigour of his understanding and character, (who, though he had formerly, with the best apparent intentions, obtained from the people the highest office in the state, yet afterwards, as if he repented of his virtues, and as if his good resolutions were profitless, grew suddenly vicious and violent, and attached himself to Marius, who, at the end of his seventieth year, was still coveting every command and every province,) this man, I say, now proposed a law to the people, by which Sylla's commission was annulled, and the conduct of the Mithridatic war decreed to Marius; to which he added other laws of pernicious and fatal tendency, such as could not be endured in a free state. He even, by means of some emissaries of his faction, put to death a son of the consul Quintus Pompeius, who was also son-in-law of Sylla.

XIX

On this, Sylla, having collected a body of troops, and returned to the city, took possession of it by force of arms, and expelled twelve promoters of these new and pernicious measures, among whom were Marius, his son, and Publius Sulpicius; at the same time procuring a law to be passed declaring them exiles. As for Sulpicius, some horsemen overtaking him in the Laurentine marshes, put him to death; and his head, being elevated and displayed on the Rostrum, was an omen, as it were, of the approaching proscription. Marius, after his sixth consulship and his seventieth year, being found naked, and covered with mud, with only his eyes and nose above the surface, among the reeds at the margin of the lake of Marica, where he had concealed himself to escape the pursuit of Sylla's horsemen, was taken out, and, with a cord about his neck, dragged to the prison of Minturnæ, by order of one of the two colonial magistrates. A public servant, by nation a German, who happened to have been taken prisoner by Marius in the Cimbrian war, was sent with a sword to despatch him; but no sooner did he recognise Marius, than, with a loud outcry, showing how much he was shocked at the fall of so great a man, he threw away the weapon, and hurried out of the prison. His countrymen, thus taught by a barbarian[20] to commiserate the man who was recently at their head, supplied him with clothes and provision for a voyage, and put him on board a ship. Having overtaken his son near the island of Ænaria, he steered his course to Africa, where, in a hut among the ruins of Carthage, he lived in a state of indigence. Here, while Marius reviewed Carthage, and Carthage contemplated him, they might afford consolation to each other.

XX

In this year the hands of the soldiers were first stained with the blood of a Roman consul. Quintus Pompeius, Sylla's colleague, was slain by the troops of Cnæus Pompey the proconsul, in a mutiny which their leader had himself excited. * * * *

Cinna showed no more moderation than Marius and Sulpicius; for although the citizenship of Rome had been granted to Italy, on the understanding that the new members should be included in eight new tribes, (lest otherwise their power and numbers might detract from the dignity of the original citizens, and the receivers of the kindness be more powerful than their benefactors,) he now promised that he would distribute them through all the tribes. With this object in view, he had drawn together into the city a vast multitude from all parts of Italy. But he was driven out of Rome by the power of his colleague and of the nobles; and, while he was on his way to Campania, the consulship was taken from him by a vote of the senate, and Lucius Cornelius Merula, flamen of Jupiter, was appointed in his place; an illegal proceeding, better suited to the demerits of the man, than for a precedent. Cinna, after first bribing the tribunes and centurions, and then gaining over the soldiers by promises of largesses, was received as leader by the army at Nola, and when all the troops had sworn obedience to him, he, retaining the ensigns of consul, turned their arms against his country; depending chiefly, however, on the vast number of the new citizens, of whom he had enlisted above three hundred cohorts, and filled up the complement of thirty legions. His party stood in need of men of character and influence; and, to add to these, he recalled from exile Caius Marius, his son, and the others who had been banished with them.

XXI

While Cinna was making war on his country, Cnæus Pompeius, father of Pompey the Great, (who had done eminent service to the state in the Marsian war, especially in the Picenian territory, and had taken Asculum, near which city, while the troops were dispersed in various other parts, seventy-five Roman citizens, in one day, maintained a conflict with more than sixty thousand Italians,) had become, from being disappointed of another consulship, so equivocal in his conduct, and so apparently undecided for either party, that he seemed to do nothing but with a view to his own advantage, and to be watching for opportunities of turning himself and his army to one side or the other, wherever the greater prospect of power for himself should appear. But at last he came to a collision with Cinna, in a long and fierce battle, of which, begun and ended as it was under the very walls and view of the city of Rome, it can hardly be expressed how grievous was the result both to the combatants and the spectators[21]. Soon after, while a pestilence was ravaging both armies, as if they were not sufficiently exhausted by the sword, Cnæus Pompeius died; but the joy felt at his death was in a great measure counterbalanced by sorrow for the loss of so many citizens, cut off by the sword or by sickness. The Roman people vented on his corpse the resentment which they owed to him when alive. Whether there were two or three families of the Pompeii, Quintus Pompeius was the first consul of that name, with Cnæus Servilius, about a hundred and sixty-seven years ago. Cinna and Marius, after several encounters, not without considerable bloodshed on both sides, made themselves masters of the city; but Cinna entered it first, and proposed a law for the recal of Marius.

XXII

Soon after, Caius Marius made his entry into the city, an entry fatal to his countrymen. Nothing could have surpassed his victorious irruption in cruelty, had not that of Sylla speedily followed. Nor was the licentious barbarity of the sword inflicted only on the middling ranks; but men of the highest stations, and most eminent characters, were destroyed under various kinds of sufferings; among these the consul Octavius, a man of the mildest disposition, was slain by order of Cinna. Merula, who, on the approach of Cinna, had resigned the consulship, having opened his veins, and sprinkled his blood on the altars, implored the same gods, whom, as priest of Jupiter, he had often intreated to preserve the Commonwealth, to pour curses on Cinna and his party, and then resigned a life, which had greatly served the state. Marcus Antonius, a man as eminent in civil dignity as in eloquence, was, by order of Marius and Cinna, stabbed by the swords of the soldiers; whom he long caused to hesitate by the power of his eloquence. Quintus Catulus, celebrated for his other merits, as well as for the fame acquired in the Cimbrian war, which was common to him and Marius, when search was made for him by executioners, shut himself up in a place lately plastered with mortar[22], had fire brought it to raise a strong smell, and then, by inhaling the noxious vapour, and holding in his breath, he found a death agreeable to his wishes, though not to the intentions of his enemies. Everything was falling headlong into ruin, but no person was yet found who dared to make a donation of the property of a Roman citizen, or to ask for it. Afterwards this additional evil was introduced, that avarice supplied motives for cruelty; magnitude of guilt was estimated by magnitude of wealth; whoever was rich, was criminal, and became a reward, as it were, for his own destruction[23]; nor was anything considered dishonourable that was gainful.

XXIII

Cinna now entered on his second consulship, and Marius on his seventh, to the utter disgrace of the former six. In the early part of it he fell sick and died, leaving a character for having been implacable in war towards his enemies, and in peace toward his countrymen, and utterly impatient of quiet. In his room was elected Valerius Flaccus, the author of a most dishonourable law, by which he obliged all creditors to accept a fourth part of what was due to them; for which proceeding deserved punishment overtook him within two years after. While Cinna tyrannised in Italy, the greater part of the nobility fled into Achaia to Sylla, and thence afterwards into Asia. Sylla meanwhile engaged the generals of Mithridates, near Athens, in Bœotia, and Macedonia, with such success that he recovered Athens, and, after expending a vast deal of labour in reducing the numerous fortifications of the Piræus, slew above two hundred thousand of the enemy, and took at least as many prisoners. If any person imputes the guilt of rebellion to the Athenians, at the time when their city was besieged by Sylla, he is certainly ignorant both of the truth and of history. For so invariable was the fidelity of the Athenians to the Romans, that at all times, and in every transaction, whatever was performed with perfect good faith, the Romans used to say was done with "Attic faith." But that people, overpowered by the force of Mithridates, were in a most miserable condition, held in possession by their enemies, besieged by their friends, and, while their inclinations were outside the walls, compelled by necessity to keep their persons within. Sylla, then passing over to Asia, found Mithridates submissive, and ready to agree to any terms whatever. He obliged him, after paying a fine in money, and delivering up half of his ships, to withdraw from Asia and all the other provinces of which he had taken possession by force of arms; he recovered the prisoners, punished the deserters and other traitors, and ordered the king to confine himself within his father's territory, that is, Pontus.

XXIV

Caius Flavius Fimbria (who, being general of the cavalry before Sylla came into Asia, had put to death Valerius Flaccus, a man that had been consul, and, having assumed the command of the army, and been saluted with the title of Imperator, had got the better of Mithridates in a vigorous engagement) slew himself on Sylla's arrival. He was a young man, who executed with bravery what he planned with utter disregard of honesty. In the same year Publius Lænas, a tribune of the people, threw from the Tarpeian rock Sextus Lucilius, who had been tribune the year before; and as his colleagues, whom he had fixed a day to bring to trial, fled in alarm to Sylla, he procured a sentence of banishment[24] against them.

Sylla, having now arranged affairs beyond sea, and having, as chief of all the Romans, received ambassadors from the Parthians, (some of whom, being magi, foretold from marks on his body that his life and memory would be glorious,) sailed home to Italy, landing at Brundisium not more than thirty thousand men to oppose two hundred thousand of his enemies. I can scarcely consider any part of Sylla's conduct more honourable than this; that while the party of Marius and Cinna held Italy in subjection, during three years, and while he never dissembled his intention of turning his arms against them, he yet did not relinquish the affairs which he had in hand, judging it right to humble an enemy, before he took vengeance on a countryman; nor was it till fear from abroad was removed, and till he had subdued foreign foes, that he proceeded to suppress opposition at home. Before the arrival of Lucius Sylla, however, Cinna was slain in a mutiny of his troops. Such a man deserved to die rather by the sentence of a conqueror, than by the rage of the soldiery. But he was a character, of whom it may truly be said, that he dared what no good man would dare, and accomplished what could be effected by none but the bravest; that he was precipitate in forming his designs, but executed them like a man. Carbo, electing no colleague in his room, continued sole consul for all the rest of the year.

XXV

It might be supposed that Sylla had come into Italy, not to take vengeance for the war raised against him, but merely to establish peace; so quietly did he lead his army through Calabria and Apulia into Campania, taking the greatest care for the safety of the fruits, lands, inhabitants, and towns; and endeavouring to put an end to the war on just and equitable terms. But peace could never be acceptable to those whose desires were unprincipled and without control. In the mean time Sylla's army increased daily; for all the best and most judicious flocked to his standard. Then, by a happy concurrence of events, he suppressed the consuls Scipio and Norbanus near Capua; Norbanus was conquered in battle; Scipio, deserted by his troops and delivered into Sylla's hands, was dismissed without injury. So different was Sylla as an adversary and a conqueror, that, while he was still gaining a victory, he was merciful to excess[25], but after it was secured, more cruel than any on record. Thus he dismissed the disarmed consul, as we have said, and released, in like manner, Quintus Sertorius, (soon to prove the firebrand of so great a war,) and many others whom he had taken; in order, we might suppose, that a proof might be seen of the existence of two distinct and opposite minds in the same person. After his victory, on the spot where, in his descent from Mount Tifata, he had encountered Caius Norbanus, he gave solemn thanks to Diana, the deity to whom that tract is sacred, and dedicated to the goddess the waters so celebrated for their salubrity and for curing diseases, with all the adjacent land. An inscription on a pillar at the door of her temple, and a brazen tablet within it, preserve to the present day the memory of this grateful religious ceremony.

XXVI

The next consuls were Carbo, a third time, and Caius Marius, son of him who had been seven times consul; the latter was then twenty-six years old, and was a man of his father's spirit, though not of his father's length of life[26]. He made many courageous efforts, nor did he, as consul, fall in any way below his name. But being defeated by Sylla in a pitched battle at Sacriportus, he retreated with his troops to Præneste, a place which was well defended by nature, and in which he had placed a strong garrison.

That nothing might be wanting to the public calamities, men rivalled each other in crimes, in a state where the rivalry had always been in virtues; and he thought himself the best man who proved himself the worst. Thus Damasippus, then prætor, during the contest at Sacriportus, murdered in the Curia Hostilia, as abettors of Sylla's party, Domitius, Mucius Scævola, who was chief pontiff, and highly celebrated for his knowledge both of divine and human law, Caius Carbo, who had been prætor, and was brother of the consul, and Antistius, who had been ædile. Let not Calpurnia, daughter of Bestia, and wife of Antistius, lose the renown of a very glorious act. When her husband was put to death, as we have said, she stabbed herself with a sword. What an accession of glory and fame to her family[27]! * *

XXVII

At this time, Pontius Telesinus, a Samnite general, a man of great spirit and activity in the field, and a thorough enemy to all the Roman name, having assembled about forty thousand young men of the greatest bravery, and the most determined obstinacy in continuing the war, maintained, in the consulship of Carbo and Marius, on the first of November, a hundred and eleven years ago, such a struggle with Sylla at the Colline gate, as brought both him and the republic into the utmost peril; nor was the state in more imminent danger when it beheld the camp of Hannibal within three miles of the city, than on that day when Telesinus, hurrying through the ranks of his army, exclaimed that the last day of Rome was come, and exhorted them in a loud voice to pull down and destroy the city, adding, that those wolves, the devourers of Italian liberty, would never cease from ravaging, until the woods, in which they took refuge, were hewn down. At length, after the first hour of the night, the Roman troops took breath, and those of the enemy retired. Next day Telesinus was found mortally wounded, but wearing the look of a conqueror, rather than of a man at the point of death. Sylla ordered his head to be cut off, and carried and displayed around the walls of Præneste. Young Caius Marius, then at length seeing his cause desperate, endeavoured to make his way out through subterraneous passages[28], which, constructed with wonderful labour, led to different parts of the adjacent country, but, as soon as he emerged from an opening, he was slain by persons stationed there for the purpose. Some say, that he died by his own hand; others, that as he was struggling with the younger brother of Telesinus, who was shut up with him, and attempting to escape at the same time, they fell by mutual wounds. In whatever manner he died, his memory, even at this day, is not obscured by the grand reputation of his father. What was Sylla's opinion of the youth, is manifest; for it was not till after his death that he assumed the title of Felix, which he would have adopted with the greatest justice, had his victories and his life ended together. The commander of the forces that besieged Marius in Præneste was Lucretius Ofella, who, having been previously a leader on Marius's side, had deserted to Sylla. The happy issue of that day, on which Telesinus and the Samnite army were repulsed, Sylla honoured with an annual celebration of games in the Circus, which are exhibited under the title of "Sylla's Games."

XXVIII

A short time before Sylla's battle at Sacriportus, some officers of his party had defeated the enemy in engagements of great importance; the two Servilii at Clusium, Metellus Pius at Faventia, and Marcus Lucullus near Fidentia. The miseries of civil war seemed now to be at an end, when they were renewed with additional violence by the cruelty of Sylla; for, being made dictator, (an office which had been discontinued a hundred and twenty years, the last having been in the year subsequent to Hannibal's departure from Italy; whence it is evident that the Roman people did not so much desire the authority of the dictatorship in times of danger, as they dreaded it in those of peace,) he used that power, which former dictators had employed to preserve the state from imminent dangers, with the unrestrained indulgence of wanton barbarity. He first adopted (would that he had been the last!) the plan of proscription; so that, in a state in which justice is granted to a hissed actor, if assailed with abusive language, a reward was publicly offered for the murder of a Roman citizen; he who procured most deaths, gained most money; the price for killing an enemy was not greater than that for killing a citizen; and each man's property became a prize for depriving him of life[29]. He vented his barbarous rage, not only on those who had borne arms against him, but on many who could not be charged with any guilt. He directed, also, that the goods of the proscribed should be sold; and the children, after being excluded from the property of their fathers, were deprived of the right of suing for places of honour; thus, what was most unreasonable, the sons of senators were obliged to bear the burdens of their station, and at the same time lost their privileges.

XXIX

Not long before Lucius Sylla's arrival in Italy, Cnæus Pompey, son of that Cnæus Pompey whose great exploits in his consulship, during the Marsian war, we have previously mentioned, being then twenty-three years of age, a hundred and thirteen years ago, began to form great projects, depending as well on his own private resources as on his own judgment, and boldly to put them in execution; and in order to support or restore the dignity of his country, assembled a strong army from the Picenian territory, which was wholly filled with his father's clients. To do justice to this man's greatness would require many volumes; but the limits of my work require that he should be characterised in a few words. His mother's name was Lucilia, of a senatorial family; he was remarkable for beauty, not such as adorns the bloom of life, but of such dignity and serenity as was well adapted to his rank and station, and which accompanied him to the last day of his life. He was distinguished for temperance, was eminent for integrity, and had a moderate share of eloquence. He was excessively covetous of power, when conferred on him from regard to his merit, but had no desire to acquire it by irregular means. In war, he was the most skilful of generals; in peace, the most moderate of citizens, except when he was jealous of having an equal. He was constant in his friendships, placable when offended, most cordial in reconciliation, most ready to receive an apology. He never, or very rarely, stretched his power to excess, and was almost exempt from vice, unless it be counted among the greatest vices, that, in a free state, the mistress of the world, though, in every right, he saw every citizen his equal, he could not endure to behold any one on a level with him in dignity. From the time of his assuming the manly gown, he was trained to war in the camp of his father, a general of consummate judgment; and he improved a genius naturally good, and capable of attaining all useful knowledge, with such singular skill in military affairs, that while Metellus received higher praise from Sertorius, Pompey was much more dreaded by him.

XXX[30]

* * * * At this time Marcus Perperna, a man who had held the prætorship, one of the proscribed, and who was of high family, but of little honour, assassinated Sertorius at a feast at Osca; and by this execrable deed procured certain victory for the Romans, ruin for his own party, and a most shameful death for himself[31]. Metellus and Pompey triumphed for the conquest of Spain. At the time of this triumph, also, Pompey was still a Roman knight; yet on the day before he entered his consulship, he rode through the city in his chariot[32]. Must it not be matter of wonder, that this man, elevated to the summit of dignity through so many extraordinary gradation of preferment, should be displeased at the Roman senate and people for favouring Caius Cæsar in his application for a second consulship? So apt are men to think everything pardonable in themselves, and to show no indulgence to others; regulating their dislike of proceedings, not by the merits of the case, but by their own wishes and feelings for particular characters. In this consulate, Pompey re-established the tribunitial power, of which Sylla had left the shadow without the substance.

While the war with Sertorius continued in Spain, sixty-four fugitive slaves, headed by Spartacus, made their escape out of a gladiator's school at Capua; and, forcibly supplying themselves with swords in that city, directed their course at first to Mount Vesuvius. Afterwards, increasing daily in numbers, they brought many and grievous disasters on the whole of Italy. At length they became so numerous, that in the last battle which they fought, they opposed forty thousand men to the Roman army. The honour of terminating this war fell to Marcus Crassus, who soon after became a leading man among the Roman people.

XXXI

The character of Cnæus Pompey had attracted the attention of the whole world, and he was regarded as something more than man. In his consulship he had very laudably taken an oath, that, on the expiration of his office, he would not take the government of any province; and this oath he had observed; when, two years after, Aulus Gabinius, a tribune of the people, got a law passed, that, whereas certain pirates kept the world in alarm with their fleets, engaging in regular warfare, and not in mere robberies or secret expeditions, and had even plundered several cities in Italy, Cnæus Pompey should be commissioned to suppress them; and should have authority in all the provinces, equal to that of the proconsuls, to the distance of fifty miles from the sea. By this decree the government of almost the whole world was vested in one man. However, a law of the like kind had been made two years before in the case of Marcus Antonius, when prætor; but as the character of the person concerned renders such a precedent more or less pernicious, so it augments or diminishes men's disapprobation of the proceeding. With regard to Antonius, they acquiesced without displeasure, for people are rarely jealous of the honours of those whose influence they do not fear. On the contrary, they look with dead on extraordinary powers conferred on persons who seem able either to resign or retain them at their own choice, and who have no limit to their acts but their own will. The nobility opposed the measure, but prudence was overcome by party violence.

XXXII

It is proper to mention in this place, a testimony to the high character, and extraordinary modesty, of Quintus Catulus. Arguing against this decree in the assembly, and having observed that Pompey was undoubtedly a man of extraordinary merit, but that he was already too great for a member of a free state, and that all power ought not to be reposed in one individual, he added, "If anything shall happen to that man, whom will you substitute in his place?" To which the whole assembly answered aloud, "Yourself, Quintus Catulus." On this, being overcome by the general concurrence of opinion, and by such an honourable proof of the public esteem, he withdrew from the assembly. Here it is pleasing to admire the modesty of the man and the justice of the people; his modesty in desisting from pressing his opinion further, and their justice in proving themselves unwilling to defraud him of a due testimony of esteem, though he was opposing and arguing against their inclinations. About the same time, Cotta divided equally between the two orders the privilege of being judges[33], which Caius Gracchus had taken from the senate, and transferred to the knights, and which Sylla had again restored to the senators. Roscius Otho now restored[34] to the knights their places in the theatre. Cnæus Pompey having engaged many officers of great abilities to assist him in the war, and having raised a navy sufficient to command every nook of the sea, very soon, with his invincible hand, freed the world from apprehension, defeated the pirates * * * in various places[35], and, attacking them on the coast of Cilicia, gave them a final overthrow. And in order the sooner to conclude a war so widely spread, he collected the remains of these depredators together, and appointed them fixed residences in towns, and in parts remote from the sea. Some blame this proceeding; but the high character of the man sufficiently justifies it; though, indeed, its reasonableness would have justified it in a man of any character. Enabling them to live without plundering, he of course diverted them from a predatory life.

XXXIII

When the war with Mithridates was drawing to a close, and while Lucius Lucullus, who, on the expiration of his consulship, seven years before, having received Asia as his province, and been appointed to act against Mithridates, had achieved many memorable exploits, having often defeated that monarch in various places, having relieved Cyzicus by a glorious victory, having vanquished Tigranes, the greatest king of the age, in Armenia, and having forborne, rather than been unable, to put the finishing hand to the war, (for though in every other respect highly deserving of praise, and in the field almost invincible, he was a slave to the desire of increasing his wealth,) while Lucullus, I say, was still prosecuting the contest, Manilius, a tribune of the people, a man always venal, and the tool of men in power, proposed a law, "that the war with Mithridates should be conducted by Cnæus Pompey." This law was passed; and a quarrel ensued between the two commanders, attended with violent altercations. Pompey reproached Lucullus with his scandalous love of money, and Lucullus railed at Pompey's inordinate ambition; and neither could be convicted of falsehood in what he laid to the charge of the other. For Pompey, from his first engagement in public business, could never with patience endure an equal, and in cases where he was entitled to the first share of honour, he wished to engross the whole; no man, indeed, being less covetous of everything else, or more so of glory. In his pursuit of employments of honour, he was immoderate; in office, he displayed the utmost moderation. Though he accepted posts of distinction with pleasure, he quitted them without regret, resigning at the will of others what he had sought for his own gratification. Lucullus, in other particulars a very great man, was the first introducer of the luxury which now prevails in buildings, entertainments, and furniture; so that, in allusion to the structures which he raised in the sea, and his conducting the sea into the land by undermining mountains, Pompey the Great used facetiously to call him "Xerxes in a toga."

XXXIV

About this time, the island of Crete was reduced under the dominion of the Roman people by Quintus Metellus. This island, under two leaders, named Panares and Lasthenes, at the head of twenty-four thousand young men, who were swift and active, patient of warfare and toil, and eminently skilled in archery, had wearied out the Roman armies during the previous three years. Even of the renown acquired here, Pompey did not refrain from seeking a share, but endeavoured to make it appear that a portion of the success was due to himself. However, their own singular merits, and the feeling against Pompey entertained by the most honourable men on the occasion, rendered the triumph of Lucullus and Metellus extremely popular.

Soon after, Marcus Cicero, who was indebted to himself for all his advancement, the noblest of new men[36], honoured in his life and pre-eminent in ability, to whom we are obliged for not being excelled in genius by those[37] whom we conquered in arms, detected, in his character of consul, and with extraordinary courage, firmness, vigilance, and activity, a conspiracy of Sergius Catiline, Lentulus, Cethegus, and other members of the senatorial and equestrian orders. Catiline was compelled, by dread of the extraordinary powers conferred on the consul, to flee from the city. Lentulus, Cethegus, and several others of great note, were, by the consul's order, under the authority of the senate, put to death in prison.

XXXV

That day of the senate's meeting, on which these transactions passed, displayed in the brightest colours the merit of Marcus Cato, which on many prior occasions had shone conspicuous, and with peculiar lustre. He was great-grandson of Marcus Cato, the founder of the Porcian family, and was a man who closely resembled virtue itself, and, in every particular of his conduct, seemed more like the gods than mankind; who never acted rightly, that he might appear to do so, but because he could not act otherwise; who never thought anything reasonable, that was not likewise just; and who, exempt from every vice, kept his own fortune always in his own power. After some had advised that Lentulus and the other conspirators should be kept in custody in the municipal towns, he, being then tribune of the people elect, very young, and almost the last that was asked his opinion, inveighed against the conspiracy with such energy and ability, that, by the warmth of his discourse, he caused the language of all that recommended lenity to be regarded with suspicion, as if they were connected with the plot; and so forcibly did he represent the dangers impending from the destruction and burning of the city, and from the subversion of the established state of public affairs, so highly, too, did he extol the merits of the consul, that the whole senate went over to his opinion, and decreed that capital punishment should be inflicted on the conspirators; and the greater part of that body, after the conclusion of the debate, escorted him to his house. But Catiline was not less resolute in the prosecution of his schemes, than he had been in forming them; for, fighting with the greatest courage, he resigned in the field of battle the breath which he owed to the executioner.

XXXVI

The birth of the emperor Augustus, ninety-two years from the present time, who was afterwards, by his greatness, to cast a shade over all men of all nations, added no small lustre to the consulship of Cicero. To notice the times at which eminent geniuses flourished during this period, may seem almost superfluous; for who is ignorant that in this age arose, separated by short intervals, Cicero, Hortensius, and, a little before them, * * * Crassus[38], Cotta, and Sulpicius, while, immediately after, appeared Brutus, Calidius, Cælius, Calvus, and Cæsar, who came next to Cicero, besides the disciples, as we may call them, of these, Corvinus, Asinius Pollio, Sallust, the rival of Thucydides, as well as the poets Varro and Lucretius, with Catullus, who was inferior to none in the style of writing which he adopted? To enumerate those that are before our eyes would seem to be but folly; amongst whom, however, the most eminent are Virgil, the prince of poets, Rabirius[39], Livy, who follows hard upon Sallust, Tibullus, and Ovid, each excellent in his peculiar species of composition. But the difficulty of criticising our living authors is proportioned to the great admiration felt for them.

XXXVII

During the time of these transactions in Rome and Italy, Cnæus Pompey was carrying on the war with extraordinary success against Mithridates, who, after the departure of Lucullus, had formed a new army of very great force. But the king being routed and put to flight, and stripped of all his forces, went into Armenia, to his son-in-law Tigranes, the most powerful prince of that age, had not his strength been somewhat reduced by the arms of Lucullus. Pompey, therefore, in pursuit of both, entered Armenia. The son of Tigranes, who was at variance with his father, was the first to meet Pompey, and soon after, the king himself, in a suppliant manner, surrendered his person and his kingdom to his disposal; previously declaring, that there was no man, either of the Roman or of any other nation, to whose honour he would entrust himself, but Cnæus Pompey; that any condition, whether favourable or adverse, which he should appoint, would be tolerable to him; and that it was no disgrace to be conquered by him whom it was impossible to conquer, nor any dishonour to submit to him whom fortune had raised above all men. The king was allowed to retain the honour of sovereignty, but was obliged to pay a vast sum of money; the whole of which, according to Pompey's constant practice, was lodged in the hands of the quæstor, and registered in the public accounts. Syria and the other provinces which he had seized, were taken from him; of which some were restored to the Roman people, and others came for the first time under its dominion, as Syria, which was sentenced to pay tribute. The limits of the king's dominion were fixed as those of Armenia.

XXXVIII

It seems not inconsistent with the plan of this work to recount briefly what states and nations have been reduced, and under whose generalship, into the form of provinces, and made tributary. This statement I shall give, that the whole history of them may more easily be learned at one view, than if each were mentioned separately. The first who transported an army into Sicily was the consul Claudius; and about fifty-two years after, Claudius Marcellus, having taken Syracuse, made it a province. Regulus first carried hostilities into Africa, about the ninth year of the first Punic war; but it was not till a hundred and five years after, (a hundred and seventy-five years from the present time,) that Publius Scipio Æmilianus, on destroying Carthage, reduced Africa into the form of a province. Sardinia submitted to a permanent yoke of government between the first and second Punic wars, through the exertions of the consul Titus Manlius. It is a strong proof of the warlike disposition of the Roman nation, that the shutting of the temple of double-faced Janus gave indication of general peace, only once under the kings, a second time in the consulship of this Titus Manlius, and a third time in the reign of Augustus. The first who led armies into Spain were the two Scipios, Cnæus and Publius, in the beginning of the second Punic war, two hundred and fifty years ago; after that, our possessions there varied, and were often partly lost, but the whole was made tributary by the arms of Augustus. Paulus subdued Macedonia, Mummius Achaia, Fulvius Nobilior Ætolia. Lucius Scipio, brother of Africanus, took Asia from Antiochus; but after it had been possessed some time by the royal family of Attalus, through the kindness of the Roman senate and people, Marcus Perperna, having taken Aristonicus prisoner, made it a tributary province. Of conquering Cyprus the honour can be given to no one; for it was in consequence of a decree of the senate, and by the instrumentality of Cato, on the death of its king, which, conscious of guilt, he inflicted on himself, that it became a province. Crete was punished, under the command of

Metellus, with the loss of its long-enjoyed liberty, and Syria and Pontus are monuments of the valour of Cnæus Pompey.

XXXIX

In Gaul, which was first entered with an army by Domitius, and Fabius the grandson of Paulus, who got the title of Allobrogicus, we often, with great detriment to ourselves, made acquisitions and lost them. But the most splendid achievements of Caius Cæsar is there conspicuous; for, under his conduct and auspices, it was so reduced, that it tamely pays almost the same tribute as all the rest of the world. By the same commander Numidia was made a province. Isauricus completely subdued Cilicia, and Manlius Vulso Gallogræcia, after the war with Antiochus. Bithynia, as we have stated, was left us as an inheritance by the will of Nicomedes. The divine Augustus, beside Spain and other nations, with the names of which his Forum is adorned, brought into the treasury, by making Egypt tributary, almost as great a revenue as his father did by the reduction of Gaul. Tiberius Cæsar extorted from the Illyrians and Dalmatians as explicit a confession of subjection as his parent had exacted from the Spaniards, and annexed to our empire, as new provinces, Rhætia, Vindelicia, Noricum, Pannonia, and the Scordisci. As he reduced these by arms, so, by the influence of his name, he made Cappadocia tributary to the Romans. But let us return to the course of our narrative.

XL

Then followed the military exploits of Cnæus Pompey, of which it is hard to tell, whether the glory or the toil was greater. In his victorious career, he traversed Media, Albania, Iberia, and then directed his march to the nations inhabiting the interior and right-hand coasts of the Pontus Euxinus, the Colchians, Heniochi, and Achæans. Mithridates, sinking under the ascendancy of Pompey, and the treachery of his own son Pharnaces, was the last of independent kings, excepting the Parthian[40]. Thus Pompey, victorious over every nation to which he had gone, grown greater than the wish of his countrymen or even than his own, and having in every way exceeded the measure of human fortune, returned to Italy. An opinion that had prevailed rendered his return extremely popular; for most people had asserted that he would not come into the city without his army, and that he would limit the liberty of the people by his own will. The more strongly they were affected by this apprehension, the more grateful was the unassuming manner in which that great commander returned; for, having disbanded his whole army at Brundisium, and retaining nothing of the general but the title, he entered the city with no other retinue than that which was constantly accustomed to attend him. During two days he exhibited a most magnificent triumph over so many kings, and, out of the spoils, brought into the treasury a much larger sum of money than had been known in any former instance, excepting that of Paulus[41]. During the absence of Pompey, Titus Ampius and Titus Labienus, tribunes of the people, got a law passed, that at the games in the Circus he might wear a crown of laurel, and all the dress usual in triumphs; and at exhibitions on the stage, a purple-bordered robe, and laurel crown; but this privilege he never thought proper to use but once, and, in truth, even that was too much. Fortune added to this man's dignity with such large increase, that he triumphed first over Africa, then over Europe, and next over Asia, rendering each part of the world a monument of his victories. But eminent stations are never exempt from envy. Lucullus, who, however, was moved by resentment of the ill-treatment shown him, and Metellus Creticus, who had a just cause of complaint, (for Pompey had taken from him some captive leaders that were intended to grace his triumph,) in conjunction with many of the nobles, laboured to prevent both Pompey's engagements to the several states, and his promises of rewards to the deserving, from being fulfilled according to his direction.

XLI

Next followed the consulship of Caius Cæsar, who arrests me as I am writing, and forces me, though in haste, to bestow some attention on him. He was born of the most noble, and, as all writers admit, most ancient family of the Julii, deriving his pedigree from Anchises and Venus. In personal beauty he was the first of all his countrymen; in vigour of mind indefatigable; liberal to excess; in spirit elevated above the nature and conception of man; in the grandeur of his designs, the celerity of his military operations, and in his cheerful endurance of dangers, exactly resembling Alexander the Great when sober and free from passion. Food he took for the sustenance of life, not for pleasure. Though he was closely connected in relationship with Caius Marius, and was also son-in-law to Cinna, (whose daughter he could by no intimidation be induced to divorce, though Marcus Piso, a man of consular rank, to gratify Sylla, had divorced Annia, who had been wife of Cinna,) and though he was only about nineteen years old when Sylla assumed the government of the state, yet the ministers and creatures of Sylla, more than himself, made search for him, in order to kill him; on which he changed his clothes, and, putting on a dress far inferior to his rank, escaped out of the city in the night. Afterwards, while he was still very young, he was taken by pirates, and during the whole time that he was detained by them, behaved in such a manner, that he became an object both of terror and veneration to them; nor did he ever, by night or by day, take off his shoes or his girdle, (for why should so remarkable a circumstance be omitted, though it cannot be told with any grace of style?) lest, if he made any alteration in his usual dress, he should render himself suspected by those who watched him only with their eyes[42].

XLII

It would require too much space to speak of all his various and numerous services, or of the conduct of the Roman magistrate, who then governed Asia, and who, through timidity, shrunk from seconding his efforts. Let what follows be mentioned, as a specimen of the conduct of a man soon to become so great. On the night succeeding the day on which he was ransomed by the public money of several states, (which, however, he managed so as to make the pirates give hostages to those states,) he collected a squadron of private vessels hastily fitted out, and sailing to the place where the pirates were, dispersed part of their fleet, sunk part, took several of their ships and men, and then, delighted at the success of his nocturnal expedition, returned to his friends. Having lodged his prisoners in custody, he proceeded to Bithynia, to the proconsul Junius, the governor of Asia, and requested him to give orders for putting the prisoners to death. This he refused, and said he would sell them, (for envy was the concomitant of his baseness of spirit[43],) when Cæsar, with incredible speed, returned to the coast, and before letters from the proconsul about the business could be conveyed to any one, crucified the whole of the prisoners.

XLIII

Returning in haste to Italy, to take on him the priest's office, (for he had been elected a pontifex in his absence, in the room of Cotta, who had been consul; and when almost a boy, indeed, he had been appointed a priest of Jupiter by Marius and Cinna, but had lost that office through the victory of Sylla, who annulled all their acts,) he embarked, in order to escape the notice of the pirates, who covered the whole sea, and were then naturally incensed against him, in a four-oared boat, with two friends and ten servants, and thus crossed the vast gulf of the Adriatic. On his passage, having seen, as he thought, some of the pirates' vessels, he threw off his gown, and fastened his dagger to his side, preparing himself for any event, but soon discovered that his sight had been deceived by a row of trees at a distance presenting the appearance of the rigging of ships. The rest of his acts in the city, his celebrated impeachment of Dolabella, to whom more public favour was shown than is generally extended to persons arraigned; his remarkable political contests with Quintus Catulus, and other eminent men; his victory, before he was prætor, and when he stood for the office of pontifex maximus, over the same Quintus Catulus, who was universally allowed to be the first man in the senate; his repairing, in his ædileship, the monuments of Caius Marius, even in opposition to the nobility; his re-instatement, at the same time, of the sons of the proscribed in the right of standing for office; his wonderful energy and activity in his prætorship and quæstorship in Spain, (where he was under Antistius Vetus, the grandfather of the present Vetus, who has been consul and is a pontifex, and who is the father of two sons that have been consuls and are priests, a man of as much virtue as human integrity can be conceived to embrace,) all these matters are too well known to require repetition here.

XLIV

In his consulship, there was settled between him, Cnæus Pompey, and Marcus Crassus, a treaty of alliance in power, which proved of fatal consequence to the city and to the world, and not less so, at subsequent periods, to themselves. Pompey's motive for entering into this plan was, that his acts in the provinces beyond sea, which were opposed by many, as we have already mentioned, might at length be confirmed by means of Cæsar, while Consul; Cæsar's, because he imagined, he should advance his own, and that by throwing on him the jealousy attending their common greatness, he should gain stability to his own strength; while Crassus was filled with the hope of acquiring, through the influence of Pompey, and the support of Cæsar, that pre-eminence which he never could attain by his own single efforts. An affinity had also been contracted by marriage between Cæsar and Pompey; for Pompey had married Cæsar's daughter. In his consulship, Cæsar procured a law to be passed, which was also supported by Pompey, that the lands of Campania should be divided among the people; in consequence of which, about twenty thousand citizens were conducted thither, and the privileges of Rome were restored to that country, about a hundred and fifty-two years after Capua had, in the Punic war, been reduced by the Romans into the condition of a prefecture. Bibulus, Cæsar's colleague, being more willing than able to obstruct his proceedings, confined himself to his house during the greater part of the year; by which conduct, while he wished to increase the odium against his colleague, he only increased his power. The province of Gaul was then decreed to Cæsar for five years.

XLV

During this period, Publius Clodius, a man of noble birth, eloquent, and daring, who knew no control for his words or actions but his own will, who fearlessly executed what he wickedly conceived, who bore the infamy of an incestuous commerce with his own sister, and who had been publicly accused of having committed adultery amidst the most solemn religious rites of the Roman people; this man, I say, being actuated by a most violent enmity to Marcus Cicero, (for how, indeed, could anything like friendship subsist between characters so dissimilar?) renounced his patrician rank, became a plebeian, was appointed a tribune, and passed a law in his tribunate, that any person who had put a Roman citizen to death without a judicial sentence, should be sent into banishment[44]. It was Cicero alone, though he was not named in this law, that was meant to be affected by it. Thus a man, who had performed the highest services to the state, received, in return for having saved his country, the penalty of exile. Cæsar and Pompey did not escape suspicion of having abetted this persecution of Cicero, who seemed to have brought it on himself by refusing to be one of the twenty commissioners for dividing the lands of Campania. In less than two years, however, by the late but intrepid exertions of Cnæus Pompey, joined with the wishes of all Italy and the decrees of the senate, and through the energy and efforts of Annius Milo, a tribune of the people, he was restored to his dignity and his country. Nor, since the exile and recal of Numidicus, had the banishment of any one excited more regret, or the return more joy. His house, which had been pulled down with great malice by Clodius, the senate rebuilt with equal magnificence.

The same Publius Clodius removed Marcus Cato from the seat of government, under pretence of giving him a very honourable employment; for he procured a law to be passed, that he should be sent in character of quæstor, but with the authority of prætor, and with another quæstor attending him, into the island of Cyprus, to despoil Ptolemy of his kingdom, who, indeed, deserved such treatment by the general viciousness of his life. But, just before Cato's arrival, he put an end to his own life, and Cato brought home from Cyprus a much larger quantity of treasure than had been expected. To praise Cato for his honesty, would be rather derogatory to him than otherwise; but to accuse him of ostentatiously displaying it, would seem but just; for when all the populace of the city, together with the consuls and the senate, poured forth to salute him as he was sailing up the Tiber, he did not disembark to meet them until he arrived at the spot where the treasure was to be landed.

XLVI

While Cæsar was achieving vast exploits in Gaul, the relation of which would require many volumes, and, not content with numerous and glorious victories, or with killing or taking great multitudes of the enemy, had at last transported his army into Britain, seeking, as it were, a new world for our government and his own, a remarkable pair of consuls[45], Cnæus Pompey and Marcus Crassus, entered on a second consulship, which they neither acquired by honourable means, nor conducted in a praiseworthy manner. By a law which Pompey proposed to the people, the government of his province was continued to Cæsar for the same length of time as before, and Syria was decreed to Crassus, who now meditated a war with Parthia. This man, in other respects irreproachable, and unstained by dissipation, knew no limits, and imposed no restraint on himself, in his pursuit of wealth and glory. When he was setting out for Syria, the tribunes of the people strove in vain to detain him, by announcing unfavourable omens; and, had their curses taken effect on him alone, the loss of the general, while the army was safe, would have been rather an advantage to the public. Crassus had crossed the Euphrates, and was on his march towards Seleucia, when king Orodes, surrounding him with an immense force of cavalry, slew him, together with the greater part of the Roman army. Caius Cassius, (who was afterwards guilty of a most atrocious crime[46],) being at that time quæstor, preserved the remains of the legions, ably retained Syria under the power of the Romans, and routed, with distinguished success, the Parthians who had invaded it, and compelled them to flee.

XLVII

During this period, that which followed, and the one which we have already mentioned, above four hundred thousand of the enemy were slain by Caius Cæsar, and a greater number taken. He fought often in pitched battles, often on his march, often made sudden attacks; twice he penetrated into Britain; and of nine campaigns, scarcely one passed without his justly deserving a triumph. But near Alesia such achievements were effected as it was scarcely for man to attempt, and for little less than a deity to accomplish. It was in the seventh year of Cæsar's stay in Gaul that Julia, the wife of Pompey the Great, died, the connecting link of concord between Pompey and Cæsar; which, through their mutual jealousy of power, had been some time in danger of disruption; and, as if fortune would dissolve every tie between leaders destined to so great a contest, the little son of Pompey and Julia died a short time after. Then, while ambition extended its rage to the sword and civil slaughter, of which neither end nor control could be found, his third consulship was conferred on Cnæus Pompey, he being made sole consul, with the approbation even of those who had formerly opposed his pretensions. In consequence of the distinction conferred on him by this election, by which it appeared that the party of the nobles were reconciled to him, the breach was greatly widened between him and Caius Cæsar. But he employed the whole power of that consulship in laying restraints on bribery. In this year, Publius Clodius was killed by Milo, then a candidate for the consulship, in a quarrel that arose on their meeting near Bovillæ; an act of bad precedent, but beneficial to the public. It was not more the feeling excited against this deed, than the will of Pompey, that caused Milo to be condemned on his trial; though Marcus Cato publicly gave his opinion in favour of his acquittal. Had he given it sooner, several would, doubtless, have followed his example, and have approved of the sacrifice of such a member of the community, than whom there never lived one more pernicious to the state, or a greater enemy to all good men.

XLVIII

In a short time after, the flames of civil war began to blaze, while every man who regarded justice wished both Cæsar and Pompey to disband their armies. For Pompey, in his second consulship, had desired that the province of Spain might be assigned to him; and during three years, while he was absent from the country, and directing affairs in Rome, he administered the government there by his deputies, Afranius of consular, and Petreius of prætorian rank; and while he assented to the judgment of those who insisted on Cæsar's disbanding of his army, he opposed those who required the same for himself. Had this man died two years before recourse was had to arms, after he had finished the structures erected at his own expense, his theatre, and the buildings around it, and when he was attacked by a violent disorder in Campania, (at which time all Italy offered prayers for his recovery, an honour never before paid to any citizen,) fortune would not have had opportunity to work his overthrow, and he would have carried undiminished to the shades below the greatness that he enjoyed in this upper world.

For producing the civil war, and all the calamities that ensued from it, through a space of twenty successive years, there was no one that supplied more flame and excitement than Caius Curio, a tribune of the people. He was of noble birth, eloquent, intrepid, prodigal alike of his own fortune and reputation, and those of others; a man ably wicked, and eloquent to the injury of the public, and whose passions and desires no degree of wealth or gratification could satisfy. At first he took the side of Pompey, that is, as it was then deemed, the side of the Commonwealth; soon after, he pretended to oppose both Cæsar and Pompey, but, in reality, was attached to Cæsar. Whether this attachment was the result of his own choice, or the consequence of a bribe of ten thousand sestertia[47], as has been said, we shall leave undetermined. At last, when salutary conditions, tending to unite all parties in peace, had been very fairly proposed by Cæsar, and were patiently considered by Pompey, this man interrupted and broke off the treaty, while Cicero laboured, with singular zeal, to preserve concord in the state. Of these and the preceding transactions, the detail is given in the larger volumes of others, and will, I trust, be sufficiently set forth in mine.

XLIX

Let my work now resume its intended character; though I would first congratulate Quintus Catulus, the two Luculli, Metellus, and Hortensius, that after having flourished in the state without envy, and enjoyed great eminence without danger, they died in the course of nature before the commencement of the civil broils, and while the state was still quiet, or at least not tending to its fall. In the consulship of Lentulus and Marcellus, seven hundred and three years after the foundation of the city, and seventy-eight before the commencement of your consulate, Marcus Vinicius, the civil war blazed forth. The cause of one of the leaders appeared to be the better, that of the other was the stronger. On one side everything was specious, on the other was greater power. The support of the senate armed Pompey with confidence, that of the soldiery, Cæsar. The consuls and senate conferred supreme authority, not on Pompey, but on his cause. Nothing was omitted by Cæsar that could be tried for the promotion of peace; to nothing would the party of Pompey listen. Of the consuls, Marcellus was more violent than was reasonable; Lentulus saw that his own security[48] was incompatible with that of the state. Marcus Cato insisted that it were better for them to die, than for the state to listen to offers from a private citizen. A man of probity and sound judgment would approve Pompey's party; a man of prudence would rather follow Cæsar's; deeming the former more honourable, the latter more formidable. At length, after rejecting every proposal of Cæsar's, the opposite party decreed that, retaining the mere title of a province, and a single legion, he should come to Rome as a private person, and, in standing for the consulship, should submit himself to the votes of the Roman people; Cæsar then resolved on war, and passed the Rubicon with his army. Cnæus Pompey, the consuls, and the greater part of the senate, withdrawing from the city, and then from Italy, sailed over to Dyrrachium.

L

Cæsar, having got into his power Domitius, and the legions with him at Corfinium, dismissed that general without delay, and every one else who chose to go to Pompey, whom he then followed to Brundisium; thus making it apparent, that he desired to put an end to war while the powers of the state were unimpaired, and negotiation open, rather than to overpower his opponents in their flight. Finding that the consuls had sailed, he returned to the city, and having represented in the senate, and in a general assembly of the people, the motives of his proceedings, and the cruel necessity under which he lay, in being compelled to take arms by the hostility of others, he resolved to go into Spain. His progress, rapid as it was, was for some time retarded by the conduct of Marseilles, which, with more honesty than good policy, unseasonably assumed the arbitration between those great men in arms; a case in which such only ought to interpose as have power to enforce submission to their award. The army, which was commanded by Afranius, who had been consul, and Petreius, who had been prætor, amazed at the energy and brilliancy of his progress, immediately surrendered itself to his pleasure. Both the commanders, and all men of every description who wished to follow them, were permitted to go to Pompey.

LI

In the year following, when Dyrrachium, and the whole country round it, were occupied by Pompey's camp, (who, by collecting about him legions from all the foreign provinces, auxiliary troops of horse and foot, and forces from kings, tetrarchs, and petty princes[49], had formed a vast army, and had, as he thought, guarded the sea with such a line of ships as would prevent Cæsar from transporting his legions,) Cæsar, proceeding with his usual despatch and success, suffered nothing to hinder him and his army from making good their passage by sea, whithersoever and whensoever he pleased. At first he pitched his camp almost close to Pompey's, and soon after shut him up within a line of circumvallation and forts. Scarcity of provisions, however, began to be felt, and more severely by the besiegers than the besieged. In this state of things, Cornelius Balbus, with a spirit of enterprise almost incredible, went into the enemy's camp, and held frequent conferences with the consul Lentulus, (who was undetermined at what price he would sell himself,) and thus opened the way for himself to those preferments, by which he (not a mere sojourner in Spain, but a native Spaniard,) rose to a triumph and pontificate, and, from a private station, became a consul. Several battles followed with various success; but one of them proved very favourable to Pompey's party, Cæsar's troops meeting a severe repulse.

LII

Cæsar then led his army into Thessaly, the destined scene of his future victory. Pompey, though his friends advised a very different course, (most of them recommending him to transfer the war into Italy; and indeed no movement could have been more beneficial to his party; others persuading him to protract the contest, a plan which, from the increasing popularity of his cause, would daily be more and more productive of good,) yet, yielding to his natural impetuosity, marched in pursuit of the enemy. The day of battle at Pharsalia, so fatal to the name of Rome, the vast effusion of blood on both sides, the two heads of the state meeting in deadly conflict, the extinction of one of the luminaries of the Commonwealth, and the slaughter of so many and so eminent men on the side of Pompey, the limits of this work do not allow me to describe at large. One thing must be observed, that as soon as Cæsar saw Pompey's line give way, he made it his first and principal care (if I may use a military expression to which I have been accustomed) to disband[50] from his breast all considerations of party. O immortal gods! what requital did this merciful man afterwards receive for his kindness then shown to Brutus? Nothing would have been more admirable, more noble, more illustrious, than this victory, (for the nation did not miss one citizen, except those who fell in battle,) had not obstinacy defeated the exertions of compassion, as the conqueror granted life more freely than the vanquished received it.

LIII

Pompey, having fled with the two Lentuli, who had been consuls, his son Sextus, and Favonius, formerly a prætor, all of whom chance had assembled in his company, (some advising him to retreat to Parthia, others to Africa, where he would find king Juba a most faithful supporter of his party,) determined at last to repair to Egypt; a course to which he was prompted by his recollection of the services which he had rendered to the father of Ptolemy, who, rather a boy than a man, was now seated on the throne of Alexandria. But who, when his benefactor is in adversity, remembers his benefits? Who thinks that any gratitude is due to the unfortunate? Or when does a change of fortune not produce a change in attachments? Men were despatched by the king, at the instigation of Theodotus and Achillas, to meet Pompey on his arrival, (who was now accompanied in his flight by his wife Cornelia, having taken her on board at Mitylene,) and to desire him to remove from the transportation into a vessel which was come to receive him. No sooner had he done so, than he, chief of all that bore the name of Roman, was murdered by the order and direction of an Egyptian slave; an event which took place in the consulship of Caius Cæsar and Publius Servilius. Such was the end of a most upright and excellent man, in the fifty-eighth year of his age, and on the day before his birthday, after three consulships and as many triumphs, after subduing the whole world, and after reaching a degree of exaltation beyond which it is impossible to ascend; fortune having made such a revolution in his condition, that he who lately wanted earth to conquer, could now scarcely find sufficient for a grave.

Of those who have made a mistake of five years in the age of this great man, who lived almost in our own times, what can I say but that they have not given due attention to the matter, especially as the succession of years, from the consulship of Atilius and Servilius, was so easy to settle? This I mention, not to censure others, but to escape censure myself.

LIV

Yet the king, and those by whose influence he was governed, showed no more attachment to Cæsar than they had shown to Pompey; for, at his coming, they made a treacherous attempt on his life, and afterwards were daring enough to make open war on him; but they soon atoned for their conduct to both these great commanders, the living and the deceased, by suffering well-merited deaths.

Pompey was no longer on earth, but his name still had influence everywhere. A strong devotion to his cause excited a formidable war in Africa, conducted by king Juba, and by Scipio, who had been consul, and whom Pompey, two years before his death, had chosen for a father-in-law; their strength being augmented by Marcus Cato, who brought some legions to them, though with the utmost difficulty, by reason of the badness of the roads, and the scarcity of provisions, and who, when the soldiers offered him the supreme command, chose rather to act under a person of superior dignity.

LV

My promise to be brief reminds me with what haste I must pursue my narrative. Cæsar, pushing his good fortune, and sailing to Africa, of which the army of Pompey's party, after killing Curio, the leader of Cæsar's adherents, had taken possession, fought there at first with various success, but afterwards with such as usually attended him, and the enemy's forces were obliged to yield. His clemency to the vanquished, on this occasion, was such as he had shown to those whom he had previously defeated. But when he had finished the war in Africa, another still more formidable demanded his attention in Spain, (as to his conquest of Pharnaces, it scarcely added anything to his renown,) for Cnæus Pompey, son of Pompey the Great, a young man of great energy in war, had formed there a powerful and formidable opposition; as multitudes, still revering the great fame of his father, flocked to his aid from every quarter of the earth. His usual fortune accompanied Cæsar to Spain; but no field of battle, more perilous or desperate, had he ever entered; for, on one occasion, when his prospect of success seemed worse than doubtful, he dismounted from his horse, placed himself before the line of his retreating troops, and, after reproaching fortune for having preserved him for such an end, declared to his soldiers that he would not retire a step; bidding then therefore consider the character and circumstances of the general whom they were going to desert. The battle was restored by the effect of shame rather than of courage; and greater efforts were made by the leader than by his men. Cnæus Pompey, who was found grievously wounded in a desert place, was slain. Labienus and Varius fell in the engagement.

LVI

Cæsar, victorious over all opposition, came home to Rome, and, what is almost incredible, granted pardon to all who had borne arms against him, and delighted the city with most magnificent exhibitions of gladiators and representations of sea-fights, and of battles with cavalry, infantry, and even with elephants; celebrating a feast, too, at which he entertained the people, and which lasted several days. He had five triumphs; the figures displayed in that for Gaul were made of citron wood; in that for Pontus, of acanthus wood[51]; in that for Alexandria, of tortoise-shell[52]; in that for Africa, of ivory; and in that for Spain, of polished silver. The money arising from the spoils was somewhat more than six hundred thousand sestertia[53]. But this great man, who had used all his victories with so much mercy, was not allowed peaceable possession of supreme power more than five months; for after returning to Rome in the month of October, he was killed on the ides of March by a band of conspirators under Brutus and Cassius; the former of whom, though he had promised him a second consulship, he had not by that means secured to his interest, and the latter he had offended by putting him off to another time. They had even drawn into their murderous plot Decimus Brutus and Caius Trebonius, the most intimate of all his adherents, men who had been raised to the highest dignity by the success of his party, with several others of great note.

Mark Antony, however, his colleague in the consulship, a man always ready for any daring deed, had excited a strong feeling against him, by placing on his head, as he was sitting in the Rostrum at the festival of Pan, a royal diadem, which Cæsar indeed pushed away, but in such a manner that he did not seem offended.

LVII

By this event was shown the excellence of the advice of Hirtius and Pansa, who had always warned Cæsar to preserve by arms the sovereignty which by arms he had to preserve by arms the sovereignty which by arms he had acquired; but he constantly declared, that he would rather die than live in constant fear of death; and thus, while he expected to meet the same good feeling that he had shown to others, he was cut off by the ungrateful men around him. The immortal gods had given him many presages and signs of his approaching danger; for the aruspices had forewarned him carefully to beware of the ides of March; his wife Calpurnia, terrified by a vision in the night, besought him to stay at home that day; and he received a paper from one that met him, containing an account of the conspiracy, but which he did not read. Surely the resistless power of fate, when it determines to reverse a man's fortune, confounds his understanding!

LVIII

The year that they perpetrated this deed, Brutus and Cassius were prætors, and Decimus Brutus consul elect. These, with the body of the conspirators, attended by a band of gladiators belonging to Decimus Brutus, seized on the Capitol. On this Mark Antony the consul convened the senate. Cassius had proposed that Antony should be killed at the same time with Cæsar, and that Cæsar's will should be annulled; but this was overruled by Brutus, who insisted that the citizens ought to seek no more than the blood of the tyrant; for so, to palliate his own conduct, he thought proper to call Cæsar. In the mean time, Dolabella, whom Cæsar had destined for his successor in the consulship, laid hold on the fasces and badges of that office; and Antony, as wishing to preserve peace, sent his own sons into the Capitol as hostages, and pledged his faith to the murderers of Cæsar, that they might come down with safety. Then was proposed by Cicero, and approved by a resolution of the senate, the imitation of that famous decree of the Athenians, enacting a general oblivion of the past.

LIX

Cæsar's will was then opened, by which he had adopted Cnæus Octavius, grandson of his sister Julia, of whose origin, though he himself has anticipated me[54], * * * I must yet say a few words. Caius Octavius, his father, was of a family which, though not patrician, was of a highly honourable equestrian rank. He possessed a sound understanding and a virtuous disposition; his conduct was distinguished by probity, and his wealth was great. In standing for the prætorship, he was chosen first among competitors of the highest character; and this honourable distinction gained him Atia, daughter of Julia, in marriage. On the expiration of his prætorship, the lots gave him the province of Macedonia, where he was honoured with the title of Imperator. On his way home to stand for the consulship, he died, leaving a son, who was under the age of manhood. This youth, who was brought up in the house of his stepfather Philippus, Caius Cæsar loved as if he were his own son; and at the age of eighteen, as he had followed him to Spain, he made him his constant companion in the Spanish war; not suffering him to use any other quarters, or to travel in any other carriage than his own; and, even while he was yet a boy, honoured him with the office of pontiff. When the civil wars were ended, in order to improve the young man's excellent capacity by a liberal education, he sent him to Apollonia to study, proposing afterwards to take him to the wars which he meditated against the Getæ and Parthians. When the news of the murder of his uncle reached him, he received from the centurions of the legions of that neighbourhood an offer of their support, and that of the troops; which Salvidienus and Agrippa advised him not to reject. Hastening to Rome, he found at Brundisium full accounts of the fall of Cæsar, and of his will. On his approach to the city, he was met by immense crowds of his friends; and when he was entering the gate, the orb of the sun over his head was seen regularly curved[55] into a circular arm, and coloured like a rainbow, as if setting a crown on the head of a man who was soon to become so great.

LX

His mother Atia and his step-father Philip were of opinion that he should not assume the name of Cæsar, as being likely to excite jealous feelings towards him; but the propitious fates of the state, and of the world, claimed him, under that name, as the founder and preserver of the Roman nation. His celestial mind accordingly spurned human counsels, determined to pursue the loftiest designs with anger rather than a humble course with safety, and choosing to follow the direction of an uncle, and that uncle Cæsar, in preference to that of his step-father; observing that it would be impious to think himself unworthy of a name of which Cæsar had thought him worthy.

The consul Antony at first met him with haughtiness, not indeed from contempt, but from fear; and after granting him an interview in Pompey's gardens, scarcely allowed him time to speak with him. Soon after, he spread malicious insinuations that Octavius was plotting against him; the falsehood of which was detected to his disgrace.

The madness of the consuls Antony and Dolabella soon burst forth into open acts of abominable tyranny. The sum of seven hundred thousand sestertia[56], deposited by Caius Cæsar in the temple of Ops, was seized by Antony, under color of false insertions which he made in Cæsar's registers[57]. Everything had its price, the consul setting the Commonwealth to sale. He even resolved to seize on the province of Gaul, which had been decreed to Decimus Brutus, consul elect; while Dolabella allotted the provinces beyond sea to himself. Between parties so discordant in their natures, and so opposite in their views, mutual hatred continually increased; and Caius Cæsar, in consequence, was exposed to daily machinations on the part of Antony.

LXI

The state, oppressed by the tyranny of Antony, lost all vigour; every man felt indignation and grief, but none had the courage to make resistance; when Caius Cæsar, in the beginning of his nineteenth year, by his wonderful exertions, and accomplishment of the most important measures, displayed, while acting in a private character, a greater spirit than the senate in support of the republic. He called out his father's veterans, first from Calatia, and then from Casilinum; and their example was followed by others, who came together in such numbers as quickly formed a regular army; and when Antony met the troops, which he had ordered to come from the foreign provinces to Brundisium, a portion of them, consisting of the Martian and the fourth legions, having learned the wish of the senate, and the abilities of Cæsar, took up their standards, and went off to join him. After honouring him with an equestrian statue, which at this day stands on the Rostrum, and testifies his age by its inscription, a compliment which, during three hundred years, was paid to none but Lucius Sylla, Cnæus Pompey, and Caius Cæsar, the senate commissioned him, in the character of proprætor, and in conjunction with the consuls elect, Hirtius and Pansa, to make war on Antony. This charge, he in his twentieth year executed with the greatest bravery in the neighbourhood of Mutina. Decimus Brutus was relieved from a siege; and Antony was forced to quit Italy in disgraceful and solitary flight. One of the consuls, however, fell in the field, and the other died of a wound a few days after.

LXII

Before Antony was obliged to flee, the highest honours were decreed by the senate, chiefly at the suggestion of Cicero, to Cæsar and his army; but, as soon as their fears were removed, their real feeling discovered itself, and their favour to Pompey's party was renewed. To Brutus and Cassius were decreed those provinces, which they themselves, without any authority from the senate, had already seized; those who furnished them with troops were commended, and all the foreign settlements were committed to their direction. For Marcus Brutus and Caius Cassius, at one time fearing the arms of Antony, at another time counterfeiting fear in order to increase the odium against him, had published declarations, that they would willingly live even all their lives in exile, if harmony could by that means be established in the republic; that they would never afford occasion for a civil war, but were satisfied with the honour which they enjoyed in the consciousness of what they had done; and, leaving Rome and Italy, with settled and similar intentions, they had, without any public commission, possessed themselves of the provinces and armies; and pretending that wherever they were, there was the Commonwealth, had received from such as were willing to gratify them, the sums of money which used to be transmitted to Rome from the foreign provinces by the quæstors. All these proceedings were recited and approved in decrees of the senate. To Decimus Brutus, because he had escaped with life by the kindness of another, a triumph was even voted. The bodies of Hirtius and Pansa were honoured with a funeral at the public expense. So little regard was paid to Cæsar, that the deputies who were sent to the army, were directed to address themselves to the soldiers in his absence. But the army was not so ungrateful as the senate; for, though Cæsar bore the affront, pretending not to notice it, the soldiers refused to listen to any directions unless their general were present. It was at this time that Cicero, out of his rooted love of Pompey's party, gave his opinion, that Cæsar was "laudandus et tollendus[58];" saying one thing while he wished that another should be understood.

LXIII

Meanwhile Antony, having fled across the Alps, and meeting a repulse in a conference with Lepidus, (who had been clandestinely made pontifex maximus in the room of Caius Cæsar, and though appointed to the government of Spain, still delayed in Gaul,) came afterwards frequently before the eyes of the soldiers, by whom, as any commander was preferable to Lepidus, and Antony, when sober, was superior to many, he was admitted at the rear of the camp through a breach which they made in the rampart; but while he took the entire direction of affairs, he still yielded to Lepidus the title of commander. About the time that he entered the camp, Juventius Laterensis, a man whose life was consistent with his death, having earnestly dissuaded Lepidus from joining Antony, who had been proclaimed a rebel, and finding his counsel disregarded, ran himself through with his sword. Plancus, with his usual duplicity, after long debating in his mind which party he should follow, and with much difficulty forming a resolution, supported for some time Decimus Brutus, (who was consul elect, and his own colleague,) boasting of acting thus in letters to the senate; but soon after betrayed him. Asinius Pollio was steadfast in his purpose, faithful to the Julian party, and adverse to that of Pompey. Both these officers made over their troops to Antony.

LXIV

Decimus Brutus, being first deserted by Plancus, and then endangered by his plots, and seeing his troops, too, gradually forsaking him, betook himself to flight, and was slain by some of Antony's emissaries, in the house of a friend, a nobleman named Camelus, thus suffering just punishment for his conduct to Caius Cæsar, to whom he was under the greatest obligations. For, though he had been the most intimate of all his friends, he became his murderer, and threw on his benefactor the odium of that fortune of which he had reaped the benefit. He thought it just that he should retain the favours which he had received from Cæsar, and that Cæsar, who had given them, should perish. It was during these times that Marcus Tullius, in a series of orations, branded the memory of Antony with eternal infamy. He, indeed, assailed Antony in splendid and noble language, but Canutius, a tribune, attacked him with constant abuse. Their defence of liberty cost both of them their lives; the proscription commenced with the blood of the tribune, and ended with that of Cicero, as if even Antony were satiated with the death of such a man. Lepidus was then declared an enemy by the senate, as had previously been the case with Antony.

LXV

A correspondence by letter was then commenced between Lepidus, Cæsar, and Antony. Hints were thrown out of an accommodation, while Antony frequently reminded Cæsar how hostile to him Pompey's party was, to what a height of power it had already arisen, and with what zeal, on the part of Cicero, Brutus and Cassius were extolled; declaring that if Cæsar disdained to come to terms with him, he would join his power to that of Brutus and Cassius, who were already at the head of seventeen legions; at the same time remarking, that Cæsar was under stronger obligations to revenge a father[59] than he to revenge a friend. Hence a league of partnership in power was concluded; and in compliance with the exhortations and entreaties of the armies, an affinity was contracted between Cæsar and Antony, the step-daughter of Antony being betrothed to Cæsar. Cæsar entered on the consulship with Quintus Pedius, on the day before he completed his twentieth year, the twenty-second of September, seven hundred and eleven years after the building of the city, and seventy-two before the beginning of your consulate, Marcus Vinicius. This year saw Ventidius assume the consular robe, immediately after wearing the prætorian, in that city through which he had been led in triumph among other Picenian prisoners. He had afterwards also a triumph.

LXVI

While Antony and Lepidus were greatly enraged, both of them having, as we have said, been declared public enemies, and while both were better pleased at hearing what they had suffered, than what they had gained, the practice of proscription, on the model given by Sylla, was, in spite of Cæsar's opposition, which was vain against the two, revived. Nothing reflects more disgrace on that period, than that either Cæsar should have been forced to proscribe any person, or that Cicero should have been proscribed by him, and that the advocate of the public should have been cut off by the villany of Antony, no one defending him, who for so many years had defended as well the cause of the public as the causes of individuals. But you have gained nothing, Mark Antony, (for the indignation bursting from my mind and heart, compels me to say what is at variance with the character of this work,) you have gained nothing, I say, by paying the hire for closing those divine lips, and cutting off that noble head, and by procuring, for a fatal reward, the death of a man, once so great as a consul, and the preserver of the Commonwealth. You deprived Marcus Cicero of a life full of trouble, and of a feeble old age; an existence more unhappy under your ascendancy, than death under your triumvirate; but of the fame and glory of his actions and writings you have been so far from despoiling him that you have even increased it. He lives, and will live in the memory of all succeeding ages. And as long as this body of the universe, whether framed by chance, or by wisdom, or by whatever means, which he, almost alone of the Romans, penetrated with his genius, comprehended in his imagination, and illustrated by his eloquence, shall continue to exist, it will carry the praise of Cicero as its companion in duration. All posterity will admire his writings against you, and execrate your conduct towards him; and sooner shall the race of man fail in the world, than his name decay.

LXVII

The calamity of this whole period no one can sufficiently deplore; much less can any one find language to express it. One thing demands observation, that there prevailed towards the proscribed the utmost fidelity in their wives, a moderate share of it in their freedmen, some portion in their slaves, and in their sons none at all; so intolerable to men is the delay of hope, on whatever grounds it be conceived. That nothing, however, should be left inviolate, Antony, as if for an attraction and excitement to atrocities, proscribed his uncle Lucius Cæsar, and Lepidus his brother Paulus. Plancus, too, had interest enough to procure a like sentence upon his brother Plotius Plancus. Among the jests of the soldiers, accordingly, who, amidst the curses of their coutrymen, followed the chariots of Lepidus and Plancus, they made use of this expression, "The consuls triumph over Germans," (that is, brothers[60] "not over Gauls."

LXVIII

Let us here mention an affair which was omitted in its proper place; for the character of the agent does not allow a screen to be cast over his act. While Cæsar was deciding by arms the fate of the empire at Pharsalia, Marcus Cælius, a man nearly resembling Curio in eloquence and ability, but his superior in both, and not less ingeniously vicious, proposed in his prætorship, as he could not be saved by quiet and moderate means, (for his property was in a more desperate state than even in his mind,) a law for the relief of debtors; nor could he be deterred from his purpose by the influence of the senate or the consul, but called to his aid Annius Milo, (who was incensed against the Julian party, because he had not obtained a repeal of his banishment,) and endeavoured to raise a sedition in the city, and secretly to stir up war in the country; however, by the authority of the senate, he was first banished, and soon after cut off by the arms of the consuls near Thurii. Similar fortune attended Milo in a similar attempt; for while he was besieging Compsa, a town of the Hirpini, he was killed by the stroke of a stone, and paid the penalty of his offences against Publius Clodius, and against his country, on which he was making war. He was a restless character, and carried his bravery even to rashness. But since I am reverting to things omitted, let me observe, that Marullus Epidius and Flavius Cæsetius, tribunes of the people, having used intemperate and unseasonable liberties in prejudice of Caius Cæsar, and having charged him with aspiring to royalty, were very near feeling the force of absolute power. Yet the anger of the prince, though often provoked, went no further than this, that, satisfied with a sentence of disgrace from the censors, instead of the punishment which a dictator might inflict, he banished them from the country, declaring that it was a great unhappiness to him, to be obliged either to depart from his nature, or suffer his dignity to be violated. But I must return to the course of my narrative.

LXIX

In Asia, Dolabella, having by a stratagem deluded Caius Trebonius, who had been consul, and with whom he was at enmity, had slain him at Smyrna. Trebonius was a man most ungrateful for the kindnesses of Cæsar, and a participator in the murder of him by whom he had been raised to the dignity of consul. In Syria, Caius Cassius, having received some legions from Statius Murcus and Crispus Marcius, who had been prætors, and were at the head of a very powerful force, shut up Dolabella in Laodicea, (for he, finding Asia pre-occupied, had proceeded into Syria,) and, having taken the town, put him to death, (Dolabella, with spirit enough, holding out his neck to the stroke of his slave,) and thus acquired the command of ten legions in that country. In Macedonia, Marcus Brutus had drawn over to his side the legions of Caius, the brother of Mark Antony, and those of Vatinius, near Dyrrachium, who willingly joined him. Antonius he had attacked in the field; Vatinius he had overawed by the dignity of his character; as Brutus was reckoned preferable to any leader of the times, and Vatinius was considered inferior to every one; a man in whom deformity of person vied with depravity of mind, so that his soul seemed lodged in an habitation perfectly adapted to it. He was seven legions strong.

By the Pedian law, which the consul Pedius, Cæsar's colleague, had proposed, a sentence of banishment had been passed on all persons concerned in the murder of Cæsar his father. At that time, Capito, my uncle, a man of senatorial rank, seconded Agrippa in the prosecution of Caius Cassius. While these transactions were passing in Italy, Cassius by active and successful operations, had got possession of Rhodes, an enterprise of extreme difficulty. Brutus had subdued the Lycians, and both of them had then marched their armies into Macedonia, while Cassius, on every occasion, acting against his nature, exceeded even Brutus in clemency. You cannot find two men whom fortune more propitiously attended, or whom, as if tired of them, she sooner deserted, than Brutus and Cassius.

LXX

Cæsar and Antony then transported their armies into Macedonia, and near the city of Philippi came to a general engagement with Brutus and Cassius. The wing that Brutus commanded, driving the enemy from the field, took Cæsar's camp; for Cæsar himself, though in a very weak state of health, performed the duties of a commander;

notwithstanding he was urged by a plain warning in a dream, not to remain in the camp. But the wing which Cassius commanded, being routed with great loss, retreated to higher ground; when Cassius, judging of his colleague's fortune by his own, despatched a veteran, with orders to bring him an account what body of men it was that were coming towards him; but the veteran being slow in bringing the intelligence, and the band of men, marching hastily up, being just at hand, (neither their faces nor their standards being distinguishable by reason of the dust,) Cassius, supposing them enemies ready to rush on him, covered his head with his robe, and intrepidly presented his extended neck to his freedman. The head of Cassius had fallen, when the veteran returned with intelligence, that Brutus was victorious; and, seeing the body of his general extended on the earth, he exclaimed, "I will follow him whom my tardiness has killed," and immediately fell on his sword. In a few days after, Brutus engaged the enemy again, and, being worsted in the field, and retreating to a hill in the night, he prevailed on Strato of Ægeum, an intimate friend, to lend him his hand in effecting his death; when, raising his left arm over his head, and holding the point of his sword in his right hand, he applied it to the side of his left breast, at the very spot where the heart beats, and throwing himself on the weapon, was transfixed by the one effort, and immediately expired.

LXXI

Messala Corvinus, a young man of shining character, who, next to Brutus and Cassius, possessed the greatest influence of any in the camp, and whom some solicited to take the command, chose to be indebted for safety to Cæsar's kindness, rather than to try any further the chance of arms. Nor did any circumstance attending his victories afford greater joy to Cæsar, than the saving of Corvinus; nor was there ever an instance of greater gratitude, or more affectionate attachment, than Corvinus showed to Cæsar in return. No war was ever more stained with the blood of illustrious men. The son of Cato fell in it; and the same fate carried off Lucullus and Hortensius, sons of the most eminent men in the state. Varro, when ready to die, predicted with great freedom of speech, in mockery of Antony, several circumstances respecting his death, which were well suited to his character, and which really came to pass. Livius Drusus, father of Julia Augusta, and Quintilius Varus, did not even try the mercy of the enemy; for Drusus slew himself in his tent; and Varus, after decking himself with all the insignia of his honours, was slain by the hand of a freedman, whom he compelled to be his executioner.

LXXII

Such was the end assigned by fortune to the party of Marcus Brutus, who was then in his thirty-seventh year, and whose mind had been incorrupt till the day which obscured all his virtues by the rashness of one act. Cassius was as much the better commander, as Brutus was the better man. Of the two, you would rather have Brutus for a friend; as an enemy, you would stand more in dread of Cassius. In the one there was greater ability, in the other greater virtue. Had they been successful, it would have been as much for the interest of the state to have had Brutus for its ruler rather than Cassius, as it was to have Cæsar rather than Antony. Cnæus Domitius, father of Lucius Domitius, whom we lately saw[61], and who was a man of very eminent and distinguished integrity, and grandfather of the present excellent youth of the same name, seized several ships, and, with a numerous train of such as chose to follow his guidance, committed himself to flight and fortune, looking for no other leader of the party than himself. Statius Murcus, who commanded a fleet, and had charge of the sea, deserted with all the troops and ships entrusted to him, and joined Sextus Pompey, son of Cnæus the Great; who, on his return from Spain, had by force gained possession of Sicily. The proscribed, whom fortune had rescued from immediate danger, flocked to him from the camp of Brutus, from Italy, and from other parts of the world; for to those who had no position in the state[62], any leader appeared sufficient, as Fortune did not give them an option, but merely pointed out a refuge; and to those who are fleeing from a destructive tempest, any anchoring-place serves for a harbour.

LXXIII

Sextus was quite illiterate, and in his language barbarous; but he was of a bold spirit, prompt to act, and quick to judge. He was a freedman among his own freedmen[63]; a slave to his slaves; envying men of dignity, to become subservient to the meanest. To this young man, who had been recalled, after Antony quitted Mutina, from Spain, where Asinius Pollio, who had been prætor, had carried on the war against him with much honour, the senate, which consisted almost wholly of Pompey's partisans, restored, at the same time that they decreed the transmarine provinces to Brutus and Cassius, the possession of his father's property, and gave him the command of the sea-coast. Having possessed himself of Sicily, as we have just said, he filled up, by receiving slaves and vagabonds into his troops, a complement of several legions; and having, by the aid of Menas and Menecrates, two of his father's freedmen who commanded his fleet, ravaged the sea with piracies and rapine, he made use of the plunder to support himself and his followers, without being ashamed to disturb with the atrocities of freebooters those seas which had been cleared of them by the arms and exertions of his father.

LXXIV

The party of Brutus and Cassius being crushed, Antony stayed behind, for the purpose of settling the foreign provinces, while Cæsar returned to Italy, which he found in a much more turbulent state than he had expected. For the consul Lucius Antony, a partaker in all his brother's vices, but destitute of the virtues which sometimes appeared in him, had, sometimes, by inveighing against Cæsar in the hearing of the veterans, and sometimes by inciting those to arms, who had not been included in the regular distribution of lands and the nomination of colonists, collected a large army. On the other sides, Fulvia the wife of Antony, in whom there was nothing feminine but the form, was throwing everything into confusion and tumult. She had chosen Præneste as the seat of war. Lucius Antony, forced to give way in every quarter to Cæsar's superior strength, retired to Perusia; while Plancus, a favourer of Antony's party, rather held out hopes of assistance than afforded him any. Cæsar, relying on his courage, and pursuing his good fortune, took Perusia, and dismissed Antony unhurt. On the Perusians great severities were inflicted, rather through the violence of the soldiers than with the consent of their commander. The city was burnt; but of this conflagration Macedonicus, one of the principal inhabitants, was the author, who, after setting fire to his house and effects, stabbed himself, and fell amid the flames.

LXXV

At the same time an insurrection broke out in Etruria, which, under pretence of serving those who had lost their lands, Tiberius Claudius Nero, who had been prætor and was then pontifex, and who was the father of Tiberius Cæsar, and a man of great spirit, accomplishments, and abilities, employed himself in fomenting. This party was dispersed and quelled on the arrival of Cæsar. Who can sufficiently wonder at the changes of fortune, and the uncertain vicissitudes of human affairs? Who must not either hope, or fear, some alteration in his present circumstances, or something contrary to what is expected? Livia, the daughter of Drusus Claudianus, a man of the highest distinction and courage; Livia, I say, the most eminent in birth, virtue, and beauty, of all the Roman ladies, whom we subsequently saw the wife of Augustus, and, after his translation to the gods, his priestess and daughter[64], was now flying from the troops of Cæsar, who was soon to be her consort, carrying in her bosom a child scarcely two years old, the present Tiberius Cæsar, the supporter of the Roman empire; and thus, passing through unfrequented roads, to avoid the swords of the soldiers, accompanied only by a single attendant, that her flight might the more easily be concealed, she made her way to the sea, and sailed, with her husband Nero, over to Sicily.

LXXVI

The testimony which I would give to a stranger, I will not withhold from my own grandfather. Caius Velleius had been chosen by Cnæus Pompey in the most honourable place among the three hundred and sixty judges; he had been præfect of the artificers under him, Marcus Brutus, and Tiberius Nero, and was a man inferior to none. Being in Campania, at the departure of Nero from Naples, whose party, through intimate friendship for him, he had supported, and being unable, from the pressure of age and weakness of body to follow him, he run himself through with his own sword. Cæsar allowed Fulvia to depart from Italy in safety, and Plancus to accompany her in her flight. Asinius Pollio, with seven legions, had long retained Venetia in subjection to Antony, and had performed many and brilliant exploits at Altinum, and in other parts of that country; and, as he was now marching forward toward Antony, he prevailed on Domitius (who, having, as we said before, quitted the camp of Brutus on the death of that general, was still undecided in his movements, and at the head of a fleet of his own,) to join Antony's party; Domitius being induced to take this step by Pollio's representations and solemn assurances. By this proceeding, whoever forms a fair judgment, must allow that no less benefit was conferred by Pollio on Antony than had be bestowed by Antony on Pollio. Antony's arrival in Italy soon after, and Cæsar's preparations to oppose him, excited apprehensions of war; but an accommodation was effected near Brundisium. About this time, the wicked schemes of Salvidienus Rufus were detected. This man, sprung from the most obscure parentage, was not satisfied with having received the highest honours, with being the next after Cnæus Pompey and Cæsar, and with having been raised from the equestrian rank to the consulship, but would even have mounted to such an height, as to see both Cæsar and the Commonwealth beneath him.

LXXVII

In consequence of the general expostulations of the people, who were sorely distressed by a scarcity of provisions occasioned by the depredations committed at sea, a treaty was likewise concluded with Sextus Pompey at Misenum; who, entertaining Cæsar and Antony on board his ship, observed with some humour, that he was giving a supper in his own Carinæ[65], alluding to the name of the street in which stood his father's house, then occupied by Antony. In this treaty it was resolved to assign Sicily and Achaia to Pompey; but with this his restless mind could not be long content; and the only advantage that his coming produced to his country was, that he stipulated for the recal and safety of all the proscribed, and of others who, for various reasons, had taken refuge with him. This stipulation restored to the republic, among other illustrious men, Claudius Nero, Marcus Silanus, Sentius Saturninus, Aruntius, and Titius. Statius Murcus, who, by joining Pompey with his famous fleet, had doubled his strength, he loaded with false accusations, because Menas and Menecrates had disdained such a man as his colleague, and put him to death in Sicily.

LXXVIII

At this period, Mark Antony married Octavia, Cæsar's sister. Pompey returned to Sicily, Antony to the transmarine provinces, which Labienus, who had gone from the camp of Brutus to the Parthians, had brought an army of that period into Syria, and had put to death Antony's deputy, had disturbed with violent commotions; but, through the courage and good conduct of Ventidius, he was cut off, together with the Parthian troops, and their king's son Pacorus, a young prince universally celebrated. Meanwhile, Cæsar, lest, in such quiet times, idleness, the greatest foe to discipline, should debilitate the soldiery, made frequent excursions throughout Illyricum and Dalmatia; and, by inuring the men to hardships, and training them in action, confirmed their strength. At this time Domitius Calvinus, being, on the expiration of his consulship, made governor of Spain, gave an instance of strict discipline, comparable to the usage of old times; for he put to death by the bastinado a centurion of the first rank, named Vibillius, for having shamefully fled in the field of battle.

LXXIX

As the fleet and fame of Pompey increased daily, Cæsar resolved to take on himself the weight of the war against him. To build ships, to collect soldiers and seamen, and to train them in naval exercises and evolutions, was the charge of Marcus Agrippa, a man of distinguished courage, proof against toil, watching, and danger; who knew perfectly well how to obey, that is, to obey one; others, he certainly wished to command: a general, in all his proceedings, averse to delay, and making action keep pace with deliberation. Having built a very fine fleet in the Avernian and Lucrine lakes, he brought, by daily practice, both soldiers and seamen to a thorough knowledge of military and naval business. With this fleet, Cæsar (having first, however, with omens, propitious to the state, espoused Livia, who was given to him in marriage by Nero her former husband,) commenced hostilities against Pompey and Sicily. But Fortune, on this occasion, gave a severe shock to him who was invincible by human power; for a storm, arising from the south-west, shattered and dispersed the greater part of his fleet near Velia and the promontory of Palinurus. This event occasioned a delay in the prosecution of the war, which was afterwards carried on with uncertain success on Cæsar's part, and sometimes with danger. For his fleet suffered severely in a second storm at the same place, and although in the first naval engagement at Mylæ, in which Agrippa commanded, the issue was favourable, yet in consequence of the unexpected arrival of the enemy's fleet, a heavy loss was sustained at Tauromenium under Cæsar's eye, nor was his person unmenaced by danger; as the legions, which had been landed with Cornificius, his lieutenant-general, were nearly surprised by Pompey. But the fortune of this hazardous juncture was amended by steady courage; for in a general engagement at sea, Pompey lost nearly all his ships, and was forced to fly to Asia, where, by order of Mark Antony, to whom he applied for succour, while he was acting a confused part between the general and the suppliant, at one time supporting his dignity, at another begging his life, he was slain by Titius; who, some time afterwards, when he was celebrating games in Pompey's theatre, was driven out by the execrations of the people, so strong had continued the detestation which he had incurred by such a deed, from the exhibition which he himself had given.

LXXX

In prosecuting the war against Pompey, Cæsar had summoned Lepidus from Africa, with twelve legions containing half their compliment of men. This man, the vainest of human beings, who merited not by a single good quality so long an indulgence of fortune, had taken the command, as he happened to be nearer to them than any other leader, of the troops of Pompey, who, however, were attracted, not by his influence or honour, but by Cæsar's; and inflated with vanity at the number of legions, which was more than twenty, he proceeded to such a degree of madness, that, though he had been a useless attendant on another's victory, which he had long retarded by dissenting from Cæsar's plans, and constantly urging measures different from those recommended by others, he yet claimed the whole credit of the success as his own, and even had the assurance to send notice to Cæsar to quit Sicily. But neither by the Scipios, nor by any of the ancient Roman commanders, was a more resolute act ever attempted or executed, than was now performed by Cæsar. For, though he was unarmed and in his cloak, carrying with him nothing but his name, he went into the camp of Lepidus, and avoiding the weapons which were thrown at him by the order of that infamous man, one of which pierced through his mantle, he boldly seized the eagle of a legion. Then might be seen the difference between the commanders. The armed troops followed the unarmed leader, and Lepidus, in the tenth year after he had arrived at a height of power not at all merited by his conduct, being deserted by Fortune and his troops, wrapped himself up in a black cloak, and, passing unobserved among the hindmost of the crowd that flocked about Cæsar, prostrated himself at his feet. His life, and the disposal of his property, were granted to his entreaties; his dignity, which he was ill qualified to support, was taken from him.

LXXXI

A sudden mutiny then broke out in the army; for when troops consider their own great numbers, they are apt to revolt from discipline, and to scorn to ask what they think themselves able to obtain by force; but it was soon quelled, partly by the firmness, and partly by the liberality of the prince. A grand addition was made at this time to the colony of Capua. Its lands were public property; and, in exchange for these, others, producing revenues of much larger value, to the amount of twelve hundred sestertia[66], were assigned them in the island of Crete; a promise was also given to them of the acqueduct, which to this day is an exceedingly fine ornament, productive of both health and pleasure.

Agrippa, for his singular services in this war, was rewarded with the distinction of a naval crown, an honour never before conferred on any Roman. Cæsar then returned victorious to Rome, and a great number of houses having been purchased by his agents, for the purpose of enlarging his own, he declared that he intended them for public uses, and announced his purpose of building a temple to Apollo, surrounded with porticos, which he afterwards erected with extraordinary magnificence.

LXXXII[67]

During this summer, in which Cæsar so happily quelled the war in Sicily, fortune changed in the east, as well to his prejudice as that of the Commonwealth. For Antony, at the head of thirteen legions, having entered Armenia and Media, and marching through those countries against the Parthians, had to encounter their king in the field. At first he lost two legions, with all their baggage and engines, with Statianus, one of his lieutenant-generals; afterwards, he himself, to the great hazard of the whole army, became often involved in difficulties from which he despaired of escape; and when he had lost no less than a fourth part of his soldiers, he was saved by the advice and fidelity of a captive Roman. This man had been made a prisoner when the army of Crassus was cut off, but as this change in his condition had produced no alteration in his feelings, he came by night to an outpost of the Romans, and gave them warning not to proceed by the road which they intended, but to make their escape through a woody part of the country. This proved the preservation of Mark Antony and his legions, out of which, however, and the whole army, was lost, as we have said, one fourth part of the soldiers, and one third of the servants and slaves; while of the baggage hardly anything was saved. Yet Antony called this flight of his, because he escaped from it with life, a victory. In the third year after, having returned into Armenia, and having, by some artifice, got its king Artavasdes into his power, he threw him into chains, which, not to fail in respect for him, he made of gold. But his passion for Cleopatra daily increasing, as well as the strength of those vices which are ever nourished by wealth, licence, and flattery, he determined to make war upon his country. Previously, however, he had given orders that he should be called the new Father Bacchus; after riding in his chariot, in the character of Bacchus, through the city of Alexandria, with a chaplet of ivy on his head, a golden-coloured robe, a thyrsus in his hand, and buskins on his feet.

LXXXIII

While Antony was making preparations for war, Plancus, not from a belief that he was choosing the right side, or from love of Cæsar or of the Commonwealth, for to both he was ever a foe, but from being infected with treason as a disorder, (having previously been the meanest flatterer of the queen, more obsequious than any slave, the letter-carrier of Antony, the prompter and actor of the vilest obscenities, venal to all men and for all purposes, and having at a banquet represented Glaucus in a dance, naked and painted green, carrying on his head a chaplet of reeds, dragging a tail after him, and crawling on his knees,) formed the resolution, on being coldly regarded by Antony, because of certain plain proofs of his dishonesty, to desert to Cæsar. He afterwards construed the clemency of the conqueror into a proof of his own merit, alleging that Cæsar had approved what he had only pardoned. Titius soon followed the example of this uncle of his. One day, when Plancus, in the senate, charged Antony in his absence, whom he had but recently deserted, with many foul enormities, Coponius, who had been prætor, and was a man of high character, observed with some humour, "Surely Antony did a great many things the day before you left him."

LXXXIV

Soon after, in the consulate of Cæsar and Messala Corvinus, the decisive contest was fought at Actium, where, long before the engagement, the victory of the Julian party was certain. On one side, both the soldiers and the commander were full of energy; on the other, everything showed want of spirit; on the one, the seamen were in full strength; on the other, they were greatly weakened by want of provisions; on the one, the ships were moderate in size and active; on the opposite, more formidable only in appearance. From the one side not a man deserted to Antony; from the other, deserters came daily to Cæsar. Besides, in the very presence and view of Antony's fleet, Leucas was stormed by Marcus Agrippa, Patræ taken, Corinth seized, and the enemy's fleet worsted twice before the final decision. King Amyntas[68], adopting the better and more profitable side, (for Dellius[69], adhering to his usual practice * * * *,) and Cnæus Domitius, a man highly esteemed, and the only one of Antony's party who never addressed the queen but by her name[70], came over to Cæsar through great and imminent dangers.

LXXXV

At length arrived the day of the great struggle, when Cæsar and Antony, with their fleets drawn up, came to a general engagement; one fighting to save, the other to ruin the world. The right wing of Cæsar's fleet was intrusted to Marcus Lurius, the left to Aruntius; to Agrippa was committed the management of the whole action. Cæsar himself, ready to go wherever he should be called by fortune, might be said to be present everywhere. On Antony's side, the direction of the fleet was given to Publicola and Sosius. Of the troops stationed on the land, Taurus commanded Cæsar's, and Canidius Antony's. When the engagement began, there was everything ready on one side, the commander, the seamen, the soldiers; on the other, nothing but the soldiers. Cleopatra first began the flight, and Antony chose rather to be the companion of a flying queen than of a fighting soldiery; and the general, whose duty it had been to punish deserters, became a deserter from his own army. The courage of his men, though deprived of their head, held out a long time in a most determined struggle; despairing of victory, they sought death in the conflict. Cæsar, wishing to soothe with words those whom he might have slain with the sword, and calling and pointing out that Antony had fled, asked them for whom, and against whom, they were fighting. At last, after a long effort in favour of their absent leader, they reluctantly laid down their arms, and yielded the victory; and Cæsar granted them life and pardon more readily than they could be persuaded to ask them of him. It was universally allowed, that the soldiery acted the part of an excellent commander, and the commander that of a most dastardly soldier. Who can doubt, therefore, whether he who took to flight at the will of Cleopatra, would, in case of success, have regulated his conduct by her will or his own? The army on land submitted in like manner, Canidius having precipitately fled to join Antony.

LXXXVI

What blessings that day procured to the world, what an improvement it produced in the state of the public welfare, who would attempt to recount in such a hasty narrative as this abridgment? The victory was attended with the greatest clemency; only a few were put to death; and these were such as would not deign to sue for mercy. From this lenity of the leader, a judgment may be formed of the limits which he would have prescribed to himself in success, had he been allowed, both at the beginning of his triumvirate and in the plains of Philippi. The faithful friendship of Lucius Aruntius, a man remarkable for integrity like that of old, was the means of saving the life of Sosius, though Cæsar had a long struggle against his inclination to spare him. Let us not pass unnoticed the memorable conduct and language of Asinius Pollio. Having, after the peace of Brundisium, stayed at home in Italy, having never seen the queen, nor, after Antony's mind was enervated by his passion for her, ever interfered in the business of his party, he replied to a request from Cæsar to accompany him to the battle at Actium, "My services to Antony are too great; his kindnesses to me are too notorious; I will therefore keep aloof from your contest, and be the prey of the conqueror."

LXXXVII

In the next year, Cæsar, pursuing the queen and Antony to Alexandria, brought the civil wars to a conclusion. Antony killed himself courageously enough, so as to compensate by his death for many faults of effeminacy. Cleopatra, eluding the vigilance of her guards, and causing an asp to be brought in to her, put an end to her life by its bite, showing no signs of womanish fear. It reflected honour on Cæsar's successes, and his merciful disposition, that not one of those who had borne arms against him was put to death by him. The cruelty of Antony took off Decimus Brutus; and the same

Antony deprived Sextus Pompey of life, though, on conquering him, he had pledged his honour to secure to him even his rank. Brutus and Cassius died voluntary deaths, without waiting to make trial of the disposition of the conquerors. The end of Antony and Cleopatra I have just related. Canidius died in a more cowardly manner than was consistent with his frequent professions. Of the murderers of Cæsar, Cassius Parmensis was the last victim of vengeance, as Trebonius had been the first.

LXXXVIII

While Cæsar was employed in putting the last hand to the Actian and the Alexandrine wars, Marcus Lepidus, a young man more amiable in person than in mind, son of that Lepidus who had been triumvir for regulating the government, by Junia a sister of Brutus, formed a plot to assassinate Cæsar, as soon as he should return to Rome. The guardianship of the city was then in the hands of Caius Mæcenas, who was of equestrian rank, but of a highly honourable family; a man who, when any affair demanded vigilance, showed the greatest alacrity, foresight, and judgment, but who, when relaxation from business could be obtained, indulged himself in indolence and pleasure to an excess of effeminacy. He was no less beloved by Cæsar, than was Agrippa, but he was not so highly promoted, because, through life, he was fully contented with the narrow purple[71]; he might have obtained equal preferment, but he had not equal desire for it. On this occasion, making not the least stir, but dissembling his knowledge of the matter, he watched the proceedings of this hot-headed young man, and then crushing him with wonderful despatch, and without any disturbance either of men or business, he stifled the direful seeds of a new and fast reviving civil war, the author meeting the punishment due to his criminal purposes. Here we may produce an instance of conjugal affection parallel to that of Calpurnia, wife of Antistius, whom we have mentioned above[72]; Servilia, the wife of Lepidus, swallowed burning coals, and thus gained immortal fame as a compensation for a premature death.

LXXXIX

How great the concourse was, and how ardent the welcome from men of all ages and ranks, with which Cæsar was met on his return to Italy and Rome; how magnificent, too, were his triumphs and donations, cannot be fully related even in the compass of a regular history, much less in so brief a work as this. There is no good which men can desire of the gods, none that the gods can bestow on men, none that can be conceived in wishes, none that can be comprised in perfect good fortune, which Augustus on his return did not realise to the state, to the Roman people, and to the world. The civil wars, which had lasted twenty years, were ended, foreign wars were suppressed, peace was recalled, the fury of arms everywhere laid asleep, energy was restored to the laws, authority to the courts of justice, and majesty to the senate; the power of the magistrates was confined within its ancient limits, only two prætors being appointed in addition to the former eight; the old and original form of the Commonwealth was re-established; the culture of the lands was revived; reverence was restored to religion, security to men's persons, and to every man safe enjoyment of his property; the old laws received useful emendations, and others of a salutary nature were introduced; and the senate was chosen without severity, though not without strictness. The principal men, who had enjoyed triumphs and the highest honours, were induced by the encouragement of the prince to add to the decorations of the city. He himself could only be persuaded to accept of the consulship, which he was prevailed upon to hold, though he made many endeavours to prevent it, for eleven years; the dictatorship, which the people resolutely pressed upon him, he as resolutely refused. A recital of the wars waged under his command, of his victories that gave peace to the world, and of his numerous works both in Italy and abroad, would give full employment to a writer, who should dedicate the whole of his life merely to those subjects. Mindful of our declared purpose, we have laid before our readers only a general view of his administration.

XC

When the civil wars were composed, as we have said, and the parts of the state, which a long succession of contests had lacerated, began to coalesce, Dalmatia, which had continued rebellious for two hundred and twenty years, was reduced to make a full acknowledgment of the Roman supremacy. The Alps, inhabited by fierce and barbarous nations, were entirely subdued. Spain, after much fighting with various success, was completely subjugated, partly by Cæsar in person, and partly by Agrippa, whom the friendship of the prince raised to a third consulship, and afterwards to be his colleague in the tribunitial power. Into this province a Roman army was first sent in the consulship of Scipio and Sempronius Longus, in the first year of the second Punic War, and two hundred and fifty years from the present time, under the command of Scipio, the uncle of Africanus; and a war was maintained there for two hundred years, with so much bloodshed on both sides, that, while Rome lost several armies and generals, the struggle was often attended with dishonour, and sometimes even with danger, to her empire. This province brought death to the Scipios; this province employed our forefathers in a disgraceful contest of twenty years with the general Viriathus; this province shook Rome itself with the terror of the Numantine war. In this province was made the scandalous treaty of Quintus Pompeius, and the more scandalous one of Mancinus, which the senate rescinded by delivering up that commander with ignominy. This province caused the loss of many generals of consular and prætorian rank, and, in the time of our fathers, exalted Sertorius to such power in arms, that during five years it was impossible to judge whether the Romans or the Spaniards were the stronger in the field, or which nation was destined to obey the other. This province, then, so extensive, so populous, and so warlike, Augustus Cæsar, about fifty years ago, reduced to such a state of pacification, that the country, which had never been free from most violent wars, was thenceforward, first under Caius Antistius, then under Publius Silius, and afterwards under other governors, perfectly exempt from the disturbances even of marauders.

XCI

While means were employed for establishing peace in the west, the Roman standards which Orodes had taken when Crassus was cut off, and those which his son Phraates had captured when Antony was driven from the country, were sent back from the east, by the king of the Parthians, to Augustus, the name which the general voice of the senate and people of Rome had, on the motion of Plancus, conferred upon Cæsar. Yet there were some who felt dissatisfied with this most happy state of affairs. Lucius Murena and Fannius Cæpio, men of different character, (for Murena, setting aside his present misconduct, might be esteemed a good man; Cæpio, even before this, had shown himself one of the worst,) formed a plot to assassinate Cæsar, but, being found guilty on a public trial, they suffered from justice that which they had intended to inflict on another by violence. Not long after, Rufus Egnatius, a man, who, in every respect, was more like a gladiator than a senator, but who, in the office of ædile, had acquired a considerable share of popularity, which he had increased by occasionally extinguishing fires with the aid of his own servants; so that from that office he succeeded to the prætorship, and afterwards had the assurance to stand for the consulate, though he was conscious of being sunk in every kind of vice and infamy; nor was his property in better condition than his mind; this man, I say, having collected a number of accomplices like himself, resolved to effect Cæsar's death, being willing to die himself, if he could but cut off the man during whose life he could not hope to prosper. For it is frequently the case, that a desperate man chooses to fall amidst public ruin, rather than to sink by himself, and desires, if he must perish, to escape notice among a multitude. But he was not more successful in keeping the secret than the former conspirators; for being thrown into prison, he suffered, with his accomplices, the death best suited to his life.

XCII

Let us not defraud of due commemoration the very meritorious conduct of an excellent man, Caius Sentius Saturninus, who was consul at this time. Cæsar was absent, being employed in regulating the affairs of Asia, and of the east, and dispensing by his presence to every part of the world the blessings of that peace, of which he was the author. Sentius, in Cæsar's absence, happened to be sole consul; and, after giving other instances of conduct distinguished by primitive strictness and the greatest firmness of mind[73], such as dragging into light the frauds of the revenue farmers, punishing their avarice, and replacing the public money in the treasury, he also, when presiding at the elections, supported the character of consul with extraordinary dignity; for whatever persons he judged unworthy to stand for the quæstorship, he forbade to declare themselves candidates for it; and, if they persisted in doing so, he threatened to make them feel the power of a consul, should they appear in the Campus Martius. And when Egnatius, elated by his popularity, conceived hopes, that as he had advanced immediately from the office of ædile to that of prætor, so he would proceed from the prætorship to the consulate, he ordered him to withdraw from the field, and, on failing to obtain compliance from him, he assured him with an oath, that even if he should be elected by the votes of the people, he would not return him. Such conduct I think comparable to any of the celebrated acts of the early consuls; but such is our nature, that we more readily bestow praise on action of which we hear, than on those which we see; we view present merit with envy, and past with veneration; thinking ourselves obscured by the one, but stimulated by the other.

XCIII

Three years before the discovery of the plot of Egnatius, about the time of the conspiracy of Murena and Cæpio, fifty years from the present time, Marcus Marcellus, son of Octavia, the sister of Augustus, (whom people generally supposed, if Cæsar should die, to be likely to succeed to his station, but suspected that that dignity would not be conferred on him without opposition from Marcus Agrippa,) died very young, after having, in the office of ædile, exhibited games with the greatest magnificence. He is said to have been a youth of excellent natural qualities, happy in temper and ability, and capable of filling the high station for which he was educated. After his death, Agrippa, who had gone to Asia under pretence of acting as deputy to the prince, but, as fame says, choosing to be out of the way during the present state of affairs, on account of private misunderstandings between him and Marcellus, returned home and married Cæsar's daughter Julia, who had been the wife of Marcellus, a woman whose offspring promoted neither her own nor her country's happiness.

XCIV

During this period, Tiberius Claudius Nero, (who, as we have said, was three years old when Livia, daughter of Claudianus Drusus, became the wife of Cæsar, being contracted to him by Nero her former husband,) a youth who had been trained in the noblest principles, who possessed in the highest degree birth, beauty, dignity of mien, valuable knowledge, and superior capacity, and who from the beginning gave hopes of becoming the great man that he now is, and by his look announced himself a prince, began to act in a public character, being made quæstor in his nineteenth year; and, under the direction of his stepfather, took such judicious measures, both in Rome and at Ostia, to remedy the exorbitant price of provisions and the scarcity of corn, that from what he did on that occasion, it plainly appeared how great he was to become. Not long after, being sent with an army, under a commission also from his stepfather, to inspect and regulate the provinces in the east, he displayed in those countries instances of every kind of virtue; and, having marched his legions into Armenia, and reduced it under the power of the Roman people, he bestowed the government of it, [which had been taken from] Artavasdes[74], on [Tigranes.] Even the king of the Parthians, awed by the fame of his great character, sent his own sons as hostages to Cæsar.

XCV
When Nero returned from those parts, Cæsar determined to try his abilities in supporting the weight of a difficult war, giving him, as an assistant in the business, his own brother Claudius Drusus, whom Livia had borne in the house of Cæsar. The two brothers attacked the Rhætians and Vindelicians on different sides, and having accomplished the sieges of many cities and forts, as well as some successful actions in the field, they completely subdued those nations, (though strongly protected by the nature of the country, difficult of access, abounding in numbers, and of savage fierceness,) with more danger than loss on the side of the Romans, but with great bloodshed on that of the enemy.

Some time before this, the censorship of Plancus and Paulus was spent in quarrelling with each other, producing neither honour to themselves nor advantage to the public; for one of them wanted the requisite capacity, the other the requisite character, for a censor. Paulus could hardly fill the office; and Plancus ought to have shrunk from it; for he could not charge young men, or hear others charge them, with any crime of which he in his old age was not guilty.

XCVI
Soon after, the death of Agrippa, who had ennobled his original obscurity by many honours, and had advanced so far as to become father-in-law to Nero, whose sons the emperor Augustus, being his own grandsons, had adopted, prefixing the names Caius and Lucius to their own, brought Nero into closer connexion with Cæsar, for Julia, Cæsar's daughter, who had been the wife of Agrippa, married Nero. The war in Pannonia, which had commenced in the consulate of Agrippa and Marcus Vinicius your grandfather, and which, raging with great fury, threatened Italy with imminent danger, was then conducted by Nero. The Pannonian nations, the tribes of the Dalmatians, the situations of the countries and rivers, the numbers of their people and the extent of their strength, the numerous and most glorious victories gained in that war by this consummate general, we shall describe in another place. Let this work preserve its character. In consequence of this success Nero enjoyed the honour of an ovation.

XCVII
But while all things on this side of the empire were conducted with the greatest success, a severe loss was sustained by the troops in Germany, under the command of the

lieutenant-general Marcus Lollius, a man who was always more anxious to get money than to discharge his duty, and, while he carefully concealed his vices, was extremely profligate. The loss of the eagle of the fifth legion called Cæsar from the city into Gaul. The change and management of the German war was then delegated to Claudius Drusus the brother of Nero, a youth of as many and as great virtues as human nature can cherish, or industry acquire; and of whose genius it is doubtful whether it was better adapted for the arts of war or of peace. His sweet and engaging manners, his courteous and unassuming demeanour[75] towards his friends, are said to have been inimitable. The comeliness of his person approached very near to that of his brother. But, when he had conquered a great part of Germany, after shedding a profusion of the blood of the inhabitants in various parts, the cruelty of the fates snatched him from the world while he was consul, and in the thirtieth year of his age. The burden of the war then devolved on Nero, who executed it with his usual valour and success; and, carrying his victorious arms over every part of Germany, without any loss of the troops committed to his charge, (an object always of great solicitude with this commander,) he subdued it so effectually as to reduce it nearly to the state of a tributary province. Another triumph, and another consulship, were in consequence conferred upon him.

XCVIII

While the transactions which we have mentioned passed in Pannonia and Germany, the military exertions of Lucius Piso, whom we behold at present the mildest guardian of the city's safety, suppressed a furious war that broke out in Thrace, where all the tribes of the nation had arisen in arms. As lieutenant-general to Cæsar, he carried on the war against them for three years; and partly by engagements in the field, partly by taking their towns, with great destruction on their side, he reduced those ferocious people to submission on the former terms of peace; by which achievement he restored security to Asia, and peace to Macedonia. Of this man, every one must think and acknowledge that his character is a composition of vigour and gentleness, and that it is hard to find any person, either more fond of ease, more ready to undergo the fatigue of business, or more anxious to despatch what is required of him, without any display of activity.

XCIX

Not long after, Tiberius Nero, having now enjoyed two consulships, and as many triumphs, having been raised to an equality with Augustus in the partnership of the tribunitian power, having become the most eminent of all his countrymen excepting one, and being inferior to him only because he wished to be so; the greatest of commanders, the most distinguished in fame and fortune, the second luminary and head of the Commonwealth, requested (out of a surprising, incredible, and unspeakable effort of affection, the causes of which were afterwards discovered, as he considered that Caius Cæsar had already assumed the manly gown, and that Lucius was now grown up to manhood, and apprehended that his own splendour might obstruct the progress of the rising youths,) leave of absence from his father-in-law and stepfather, that he might rest from a continual course of labours, but without discovering the true reasons for such a resolution. An account of the sentiments of the people on this occasion, of the feelings of individuals, of the tears shed by every one on taking leave of this great man, and how near his country was to insisting on his stay, must be reserved for my history at large. But one thing must be mentioned even in this hasty narration; that he spent seven years at Rhodes in such a manner, that all proconsuls and legates going into the transmarine provinces waited on him there with compliments, lowering their fasces to him always even in his private character, (if such majesty was ever private,) and acknowledging his retirement more to be respected than their high employments.

C

The whole world was sensible that Nero had withdrawn from the guardianship of the city. Not only the Parthians, renouncing their alliance of Rome, laid their hands on Armenia; but Germany, when the eyes of its conqueror were turned away, rose up in rebellion. But in the city, in that same year, (thirty from the present time,) in which the emperor Augustus, being consul with Caninius Gallus, gratified the eyes and minds of the Roman people, on occasion of dedicating a Temple to Mars, with most magnificent spectacles of gladiators and a sea-fight, a calamity disgraceful to mention, and dreadful to call to mind, fell upon his own house. His daughter Julia, utterly regardless of the dignity of her father and husband, indulged in every excess which a woman can practice or allow at the instigation of luxury and libidinousness, measuring her license to be vicious by the eminence of her station, and pronouncing everything lawful that gratified her desires. On this occasion Julius Antonius[76], who from being a conspicuous example of Cæsar's mercy became a violator of his house, was himself the avenger of his own guilt. To this man, after the overthrow of his father, Cæsar had granted not only life, but a priest's office, a prætorship, a consulate, and the government of provinces, and had even admitted him to the closest affinity, by giving him in marriage the daughter of his own sister. And Quintius Crispinus, who covered exorbitant wickedness under a morose austerity of countenance, with Appius Claudius, Sempronius Gracchus, Scipio, and others of less note, of both orders, suffered only such punishment as they would have incurred for corrupting any ordinary person's wife; though they had defiled the daughter of Cæsar, and wife of Nero. Julia was banished to the island [of Pandataria], and thus removed from the sight of her country and her parents; though, indeed, her mother Scribonia accompanied her, and remained a voluntary sharer in her exile.

CI

A short time had intervened, when Caius Cæsar, after making a progress through other provinces to inspect their condition, was sent to Syria, and made, on his way, a visit to Tiberius Nero, paying every mark of respect to him as to a superior; but, during his stay in the province, his conduct was so variable, that neither would abundant matter be wanting to him who would praise it, nor a sufficiency to him who would censure it. This noble youth had an interview with the king of the Parthians in an island of the Euphrates, each having an equal number of attendants. This grand and memorable spectacle, of the Roman army standing on one side, and the Parthian on the other, while the most illustrious heads of the greatest empires in the world held their meeting, I had the good fortune to behold, soon after my entrance into the army, being then a military tribune. This rank I attained, Marcus Vinicius, while serving under your father and Publius Silius in Thrace and Macedonia; and having since seen Achaia, Asia, all the provinces in the east, and the mouth and both shores of the Pontic sea, I now receive much pleasure from the recollection of so many events, places, nations, and cities. The Parthian was first entertained at a banquet by Caius, on our bank; then Caius by the king, on the bank opposite.

CII

On this occasion, some treacherous schemes, full of artifice and deceit, which had been formed by Marcus Lollius, whom Augustus had chosen director of the youth of his son, were revealed to Cæsar by the Parthian prince; and they were afterwards made public by common fame. Whether Lollius's death, which followed in a few days, was fortuitous or voluntary, I have not discovered; but the joy, which people felt at his decease, was counterbalanced by their grief for the loss of Censorinus, who died soon after in the same province, a man formed by nature to captivate the affections of mankind. Caius then marched into Armenia, and, at the beginning, conducted nearly everything well; but afterwards, in a conference near Artigera, where he had rashly exposed himself, being severely wounded by a man named Adduus, he became, in consequence, less active in body, and mentally less capable of benefiting the public. He had about him, also, a crowd of courtiers, who encouraged his vices by adulation; for flattery is always attendant on high station, and, by this means, he was so far perverted, that he wished to spend his life in the most retired and distant corner of the globe, rather than return to Rome. However, after many struggles he consented, and having reluctantly set out for Italy, he fell sick and died at a town in Lycia, which they called Limyra. His brother, Lucius Cæsar, had died a year before at Marseilles, as he was going to Spain.

CIII

But Fortune, though she had frustrated the hopes entertained of those illustrious names, had already restored to the republic its own peculiar safeguard. For before the death of either, Tiberius Nero coming home from Rhodes, in the consulate of Publius Vicinius, your father, had filled his country with incredible joy. Augustus Cæsar did not long hesitate as to his adoption; not having to seek one whom he might elect, but to elect him who was most worthy. What he had purposed, therefore, after the death of Lucius, while Caius was yet alive, but had been diverted from doing by the earnest opposition of Nero, he, on the decease of the two young men, determined to execute; and accordingly constituted Nero his partner in the tribunician power, though the latter used many arguments against the measure, both at home and in the senate; and moreover, in the consulship of Ælius Catus and Sentius, seven hundred and fifty-seven years after the building of the city, twenty-seven from the present time, and on the twenty-seventh of June, he adopted him as his son. The joy of that day, the concourse of all ranks of men, the prayers offered by people stretching their hands, as it were, up to heaven itself, and the hopes then conceived of perpetual security, and of the eternal duration of the Roman empire, we shall scarcely be able to represent fully in our large work, much less can we attempt to do justice to them here. I must be content with observing that he was all in all to every one[77]. Then shone forth to parents a certain hope of security for their children, to husbands of provision for their wives, to landowners of retaining their patrimony, and to all men, of safety, quiet, peace, and tranquillity; so that nothing further could be hoped, nor could hope have a happier prospect of fulfilment.

CIV

On the same day he adopted Marcus Agrippa, of whom Julia was delivered after Agrippa's death. But in the adoption of Nero an addition was made to the formula in these very words of Cæsar: "This I do for the good of the Commonwealth." His country did not long detain in the city the champion and guardian of its empire, but speedily sent him into Germany, where a most violent war had broken out three years before, when Marcus Vinicius, your grandfather, a man of the highest reputation, was governor there, who had engaged the enemy in some places, and in others had made an honourable defence; for which merits triumphal ornaments were decreed him, with a noble inscription reciting his performances. This year made me a soldier in the camp of Tiberius Cæsar, having previously held the office of tribune. For shortly after his adoption, being sent with him into Germany in the post of præfect of cavalry, succeeding my father in that office, I was, for nine successive years, either as præfect, or lieutenant-general, a spectator, and, as far as the mediocrity of my ability allowed, an assistant in his glorious achievements. Nor do I think that any human being can have an opportunity of enjoying another spectacle like that which I enjoyed, when, throughout the most populous part of Italy, and the whole length of the Gallic provinces, the people, on seeing again their former commander, who in merit and power was Cæsar, before he was so in name, congratulated themselves even more warmly than they congratulated him. At the very sight of him, tears of joy sprung from the eyes of the soldiers, and there appeared in their salutations an unusual degree of spirit, a kind of exultation, and an eager wish to touch his hand. Nor could they restrain themselves from adding, "General, we see you, we once more receive you in safety;" and again, "General, I was with you in Armenia," "I in Rhætia," "I was rewarded by you in Vindelicia," "I in Pannonia," "I in Germany;" all this cannot be described in words, and perhaps will scarcely gain belief.

CV

Germany was entered without delay; the Caninefates, the Attuarii, the Bructeri, were subdued; the Cherusci were again received into submission; the river Visurgis, afterwards rendered remarkable by a disaster of our troops, was crossed; the parts beyond it were penetrated; while Cæsar assumed to himself all the most laborious and dangerous parts of the war, employing, in those which were attended with less hazard, the services of Sentius Saturninus, who was then his father's deputy in Germany; a man of manifold virtues, diligent, active, provident, able to sustain military duties, as well as eminently skilled in them; but who, when business gave place to leisure, wasted his time in expensive indulgences, yet in such a manner, that he might rather be called splendid and gay, than luxurious or indolent. Of his meritorious and celebrated consulship we have already spoken. The campaign of that year was protracted to the month of December, and rewarded our exertions with abundant success. His filial affection drew Cæsar to Rome, though the Alps were rendered almost impassable by the winter; but in the beginning of spring the necessity of protecting the empire recalled him to Germany, in the heart of which country, at the source of the river Lupia[78], the general at his departure had fixed his winter quarters.

CVI

Good gods! For how large a volume did we achieve sufficient exploits in the following summer, under the command of Tiberius Cæsar! The whole extent of Germany was traversed by our army; nations were conquered that were almost unknown to us even in name. The tribes of the Cauchians were reduced to submission; all their youth, infinite in number, gigantic in size, strongly guarded by the nature of the country, delivered up their weapons, and, with their leaders, surrounded by troops of our soldiers glittering in arms, prostrated themselves before the general's tribunal. The Longobardi, a nation exceeding even the Germans in fierceness, were crushed. In fine, what had never before been hoped, much less attempted, the Roman army carried its standards to the distance of four hundred miles from the Rhine, as far as the Elbe, which flows along the borders of the Semnones and Hermunduri; and, by singular good fortune, the care of the general, and a proper attention to the seasons, a fleet which had sailed round the bays of the Ocean, came from a sea, previously unheard of and unknown, up the Elbe to the same place, and, crowned with victory over many nations, and supplied with a vast abundance of all things, joined Cæsar and his army.

CVII

I cannot forbear inserting the following incident, whatever may be thought of it, among affairs of so much greater magnitude. While we were encamped on the hither bank of the last-mentioned river, and while the farther bank glittered with the armour of the enemy's troops, who, be it observed, one of the barbarians, far advanced in years, of extraordinary stature, and, as his dress indicated, of the highest dignity, embarked in a canoe formed of a tree hollowed out, such as is common among those nations; and, managing this vessel alone, he advanced as far as the middle of the stream, requesting to be allowed, without danger to himself, to land on the bank which we occupied with our army, and to see Cæsar. This request was granted. Having then brought his canoe to the shore, and contemplated Cæsar a long time in silence, he said, "Our young men are certainly mad; they worship your divinity in your absence; yet, in you presence, choose rather to dread your arms, than to trust your faith. For my part, Cæsar, I have this day, by your permission and favour, seen the gods, of whom I had before only heard, and I never in my life either wished for, or experienced, a day of greater happiness." Then, having obtained leave to touch his hand, he re-embarked in his little vessel, and continually looking back at Cæsar, sailed away to the bank occupied by his countrymen. Victorious over every nation and place that he had approached, Cæsar, with his army safe and unimpaired, for it had been only once attacked, and then by a stratagem on the part of the enemy, and with great loss to themselves, led back his legions to winter quarters, and returned to Rome with as much haste as he had used in the preceding year.

CVIII

Nothing now remained to be conquered in Germany, except the nation of the Marcomanni, who, under the command of Maroboduus, had forsaken their original abode, and having retired into the interior parts of the country, now dwelt in plains surrounded by the Hercynian forest. No haste could be an excuse for passing this chieftain without notice. Maroboduus was of distinguished birth, of great bodily strength, of a bold, daring spirit, and though a barbarian by birth, was no barbarian in understanding. He held a sovereignty over his nation, not gained by party struggles or by chance, nor variable at the will of his subjects, but steady and firmly established; and animated by a kingly spirit, he determined to lead away his people far from the Romans, and to proceed to some place, where, being beyond the reach of more powerful arms, he might render his own supreme.

CIX

Accordingly, having taken possession of the country above mentioned, he brought all the neighbouring tribes under his dominion, either by force, or on terms of agreement. He had a guard for the protection of his person; and his army being brought, by continual practice, to a close resemblance to the discipline of the Romans, he advanced his power to such a height as to become formidable even to our empire. Towards the Romans he so conducted himself, that, though he did not attack us, he plainly showed, that if he should be attacked, he had abundance of strength and inclination to make resistance. The ambassadors, whom he sent to the Cæsars, sometimes presented his respects, as if he were their humble suppliant, and sometimes spoke for him as their equal. For nations and individuals revolting from us, there was with him a safe refuge; and he acted the part, wholly or with but little dissimulation, of a rival. His army, which he had raised to seventy thousand foot, and four thousand horse, he prepared, by constant exercise in warfare against his neighbours, for more important business than he had then in hand. He was formidable likewise on this account, that having Germany on his left and front, Pannonia on the right, and Noricum at the back of his territory, he was dreaded by them all, as being always ready to attack them. Nor did he allow Italy to be unconcerned at the growth of his power; for the frontier of his dominions was distant little more than two hundred miles from the summit of the Alps, which form the boundary of Italy. This man and his country, Tiberius Cæsar resolved to attack in the following year, on different sides. Sentius Saturninus was accordingly directed, after cutting a passage through the Hercynian forest, to march his legions through the Catti to Boiohœmum, (so the country of Maroboduus is called,) and Cæsar himself proceeded to lead the army, which was then serving in Illyricum against the Marcomanni, by the way of Carnuntum, the nearest place in the kingdom of Noricum on that side.

CX

Fortune sometimes frustrates, sometimes retards, the purposes of men. Cæsar had already prepared winter quarters on the Danube, had brought his army within five days' march of the enemy's frontier, and had ordered Saturninus to bring up his forces, (which were at nearly an equal distance from the enemy, and were ready to form a junction with Cæsar in a few days, at the place already mentioned[79],) when the whole of Pannonia, which had become impatient of control from long enjoyment of peace, and Dalmatia, now grown up to full strength, having drawn into a confederacy all the nations of that region, took up arms in concert. The commands of necessity were consequently preferred to the call of glory; for it was not thought safe to keep the army at such a distance in the interior country, and leave Italy open to an enemy so near it. Of the states and nations which rose in insurrection, the number of men amounted to more than eight hundred thousand; two hundred thousand foot were assembled, well appointed with arms, and nine thousand horse. Of this immense multitude, commanded by very active and able leaders, one part was intended to march against Italy, which joins their country at the confines of Nauportum and Tergeste; another part had already made an irruption into Macedonia, and a third was appointed to guard their own countries. The chief command was vested in three leaders, the two Batones and Pinnes. With regard to the Pannonians, they had all some knowledge, not only of the discipline, but also of the language of the Romans; and most of them understood something of letters, and were no strangers to exercises of the mind. No other nation ever entered on war so soon after resolving on it, or so speedily put its determinations in execution. Roman citizens were murdered, traders slain, and, in that quarter of the country most remote from the general, a vast number of soldiers[80] cut off. All Macedonia was reduced by their arms, and everything in every part wasted with fire and sword. So powerful, indeed, were the apprehensions excited by this war, that they shook and alarmed even the steady mind of Augustus Cæsar, strengthened as it was by experience in wars of such magnitude.

CXI

Troops were accordingly levied; all the veterans were everywhere called out; and not only men, but women, were compelled to furnish freedmen for soldiers, in proportion to their income. The prince was heard to say in the senate, that, unless they were on their guard, the enemy might in ten days come within sight of the city of Rome. The services of Roman senators and knights were required, according to their promises, in support of the war. But all these preparations we should have made in vain, had there been no one to direct. The Commonwealth, therefore, requested of Augustus to give the command in that war to Tiberius, as their best defender.

61

In this war, likewise, my humble ability found a post of honourable employment. After completing my service in the cavalry, and being appointed quæstor, and, though not yet a senator, set on an equal footing with senators, and with the tribunes of the people elect[81], I led from the city a detachment of the army, intrusted to me by Augustus, to join his son. Then, in my quæstorship[82], having given up my chance of a province, I was sent by Augustus as his legate to his son; and what prodigious armies of the enemy did we behold[83] in that first year! What opportunities did we improve, through the wisdom of our leader, so as to exhaust the fury of their whole force by dividing it! With what attention[84] to the convenience of the men did we see business managed, under the orders of the commander! With what wisdom were the winter quarters regulated! How laboriously was the enemy surrounded with guards of our troops, so that they might not make their way out, but, destitute of provisions, and raging in their confinement, might waste their spirit and their strength!

CXII

An exploit of Messalinus, in the first campaign of this war, happy in the issue, as well as resolute in the effort, deserves to be recorded. This man, more noble in spirit than even in birth, most worthy of having Corvinus for his father, and of leaving his surname to his brother Cotta, being appointed to command in Illyricum, and, in a sudden insurrection, being surrounded by an army of the enemy, and having with him only the twentieth legion, which had then but half its complement of men, routed and put to flight a force of twenty thousand; an achievement for which he was honoured with triumphal decorations.

So little confidence had the barbarians in their numbers, and so little reliance on their strength, that wherever Cæsar appeared, they could not be sure of making any effectual effort against him. The division of their army opposed to him, being cut off from provisions at our pleasure or convenience, and reduced to mortal famine, and neither daring to withstand us when we assailed them, nor to engage with us when we offered battle and drew up in line before them, took post at last on mount Claudius, and protected themselves with a fortification. But another division, which had poured out to meet an army brought from the transmarine provinces by Aulus Cæcina and Plautius Silvanus, both of whom had been consuls, surrounding five of our legions, with the auxiliary troops and royal cavalry, (for Rhæmetalces, king of Thrace, had joined these two generals, bringing a large body of Thracians to assist in the war,) gave them such a blow as had nearly proved fatal to them all. The king's cavalry was routed; the horse of the allies put to flight; the cohorts were forced to retreat; and even at the standards of the legions[85] some confusion took place. But the courage of the Roman soldiers, on that occasion, gained them more honour than they left to their officers, who, widely differing from the practice of the commander-in-chief, found themselves in the midst of the enemy, before they had ascertained from their scouts in which direction they lay. In this perilous emergency, (when some of the military tribunes were slain, with one prefect of the camp, and some prefects of the cohorts, the centurions, also, not having escaped, for some of the first rank were killed,) the legions, encouraging one another, made a charge upon the enemy, and, not content with standing their ground against them, broke their line, and gained an unexpected victory.

About this time, Agrippa[86], who had been adopted by his natural grandfather, on the same day with Tiberius, and had in the two last years begun to discover his real character, plunging into profligacy with extraordinary depravity of mind and feeling, alienated from himself the affection of his father by adoption, who was also his grandfather[87]; and soon after, sinking every day deeper into vice, he met an end suitable to the madness of his conduct.

CXIII

You may now, Marcus Vinicius, conceive Cæsar as great in the character of a leader in war, as you see him in that of a prince in peace. When he had united his forces, those under his immediate command, and those who had joined him as auxiliaries, and had brought into one camp ten legions, more than seventy auxiliary cohorts, fourteen squadrons of horse, more than ten thousand veterans, a great number of volunteers, and the numerous cavalry of the king, (in short, so great an army, as had never been seen in one place since in the civil wars,) every one was rejoiced at the sight, feeling the utmost confidence of success from their numbers. But the general, the best judge of his own proceedings, preferring the advantageous to the showy, and, as I always saw him act in every war, pursuing what was eligible in itself, not what was generally recommended, having allowed the army that had joined him to rest a few days, to recruit the strength of the men after their march, and having decided that it rendered his force too large to be kept in order, and too unwieldly to be properly managed, he resolved to send it away; and, after accompanying it through a long and most fatiguing march, the difficulty of which can hardly be described, (in order that as none would venture to attack the whole, so the whole, each nation from apprehension for its own territories, might abstain from attacking either of the parties on their separation,) he sent it back to the parts from which it came, and returning himself to Siscia[88], in the beginning of a very severe winter, appointed lieutenant-generals, of whom I was one, to command the several divisions in winter quarters.

CXIV

His conduct was truly amazing, not ostentatious, but distinguished by real and solid virtue and usefulness, most delightful to experience, most exemplary in its humanity. During the whole time of the German and Pannonian wars, not one of us, or of those who preceded or followed our steps, was at any time sick, but his recovery and health were promoted by Cæsar with as much care, as if his thoughts, which were obliged to attend to such an infinite variety of laborious business, had no employment but this alone. There was a carriage kept always in readiness for such as wanted it, and a litter for general use, of which I, as well as others, experienced the benefit. Physicians, too, proper kinds of food, and the warm bath, introduced for that sole purpose, contributed to the health of all. Houses and domestics, indeed, were wanting, but no accommodation that could either be afforded or desired in them. To this I shall add what every one, who was present on the occasions, will readily acknowledge to be true, as well as the other circumstances that I have mentioned. The general alone always travelled on horseback[89]; he alone, with those whom he invited during the greater part of the summer campaigns, sat at meals[90]. To such as forbore to follow this strict mode of living, he was very indulgent, provided they did no harm by their example; he frequently admonished and reproved, very rarely punished; acting a middle part, dissembling his knowledge of most faults, and preventing the commission of others. The winter contributed much to bring the war to a conclusion. In the following summer, all Pannonia begged for peace; so that the remains of war were confined to Dalmatia. So many thousands of brave men who had lately threatened Italy with slavery, surrendering their arms, (which they had employed at the knees of Cæsar, together with Bato and Pines, leaders of high reputation, one captive, the other submitting, formed a scene which I hope to describe at large in my regular history. In autumn, the victorious army was led back into winter quarters; and the command in chief of all the troops was given by Cæsar to Marcus Lepidus, a man in fame and fortune nearest to the Cæsars; and every one, the longer and better he knows and becomes acquainted with him, the more he loves and admires him, and acknowledges him to be a credit to the great names from which he is descended.

CXV

Cæsar now turned his thoughts and arms to the remaining part of the war in Dalmatia; in which country, how useful an assistant and lieutenant-general he found in my brother, Magius Celer Velleianus, is testified by his own and his father's declaration; and the record of the high honours conferred on him by Cæsar at his triumph, confirms it. In the beginning of the summer, Lepidus, having drawn out the army from winter quarters, and making his way to join his general Tiberius, through nations unimpaired in strength, still free from the calamities of war, and, in consequence, daring and ferocious, he succeeded, after struggling with the difficulty of the passes, and the force of the enemy, and making great havoc of those who opposed him, cutting down their corn, burning their houses, and slaughtering their men, in reaching the quarters of Cæsar, before whom he appeared exulting with victory and laden with spoil. In reward for these services, which, if performed on his own account, would have entitled him to a triumph, he was honoured with the judgment of the princes. That summer brought this important war to a conclusion, for the Perustæ and Desitiates of Dalmatia, notwithstanding that they were almost impregnably secured by their mountainous countries, by the fierceness of their temper, by their surprising military skill, and more especially by the narrow passes of their forests, were at length, after being brought to the utmost extremities, reduced to quiet, not by the orders, but by the arms and personal exertions, of Cæsar himself. In all this great war in Germany, I could observe nothing more noble, nothing more deserving of admiration, than that the general never thought any opportunity of success so attractive as to justify a squandering of the lives of his soldiers; he ever judged the safest means the most honourable, and preferred the approbation of his conscience to the acquisition of fame; nor were the counsels of the general ever swayed by the feelings of the army, but the army was always guided by the wisdom of the general.

CXVI

In the Dalmatian war, Germanicus, being sent forward into various places with difficulty and danger, exhibited great proofs of courage; and Vibius Postumius, who had been consul, and was governor of Dalmatia, obtained, by his activity and diligence in the service, the distinction of triumphal decorations; which honour, a few years before, Passienus and Cossus, men celebrated for certain virtues of opposite kinds, had attained in Africa. But Cossus converted this testimony of his success into a surname for his son[91], a youth formed by nature as a pattern of every virtue. Lucius Apronius, who shared in the actions of Postumus, merited, by his excellent conduct in that service, those honours which he afterwards obtained. I wish that it were not proved by more remarkable instances how much Fortune rules in everything; but in cases of this kind her power may be abundantly recognised; for Ælius Lamia, a man of primitive manners, who always tempered with humanity the severity of old times, failed, after discharging the most honourable employments in Germany, Illyricum, and Africa, not of deserving, but of an opportunity of obtaining triumphal honours. Aulus Licinius Nerva Silanus, too, son of Publius Silius, a man whom not even those who knew him could sufficiently admire, was prematurely snatched away by fate, (all the hopes of an excellent citizen and most upright commander being cut off,) and prevented from enjoying the fruit of the prince's distinguished friendship, and from attaining a height of exultation as lofty as that of his father. If any one shall say that I looked for a place for mentioning these men, he will but charge me with what I readily admit; for candidly to do justice, without exceeding the truth, is no subject of accusation in the eyes of the right-minded.

CXVII

Cæsar had but just concluded the war in Pannonia and Dalmatia, when, within five days after the final termination of it, mournful news [arrived[92]] from Germany; that Varus was killed, three legions cut to pieces, as many troops of cavalry, and six cohorts; the only favour allowed to us by Fortune being, that [this calamity did not happen] while the commander-in-chief was still engaged [in the Dalmatic war, when the rebellious Germans might have formed a junction with the enemy in that country.] But the occasion, and the character of the leader, demand some attention. Quintilius Varus was born of a noble rather than illustrious family, was of a mild disposition, of sedate manners, and, being somewhat indolent as well in body as in mind, was more accustomed to ease in a camp than to action in the field. How far he was from despising money, Syria, of which he had been governor, afforded proof; for, going a poor man into that rich province, he became a rich man, and left it a poor province. Being appointed commander of the army in Germany, he imagined that the inhabitants had nothing human but the voice[93] and limbs, and that men who could not be tamed by the sword, might be civilised by law. With this notion, having marched into the heart of Germany, as if among people who delighted in the sweets of peace, he spent the summer in deciding controversies, and ordering the pleadings before a tribunal.

CXVIII

But those people, though a person unacquainted with them would hardly believe it, are, while extremely savage, exquisitely artful, a race, indeed, formed by nature for deceit; and, accordingly, by sometimes prosecuting each other for pretended injuries, and then returning thanks for the decision of these suits by Roman equity, for the civilisation of their barbarous state by this new system, and for the termination by law of disputes which used to be decided by arms, they at length lulled Quintilius into such a perfect feeling of security, that he fancied himself a city prætor dispensing justice in the forum, instead of the commander of an army in the middle of Germany. It was at this time that a youth of illustrious birth, the son of Segimer, prince of that nation, named Arminius, brave in action, quick in apprehension, and of activity of mind far beyond the state of barbarism, showing in his eyes and countenance the ardour of his feelings, (a youth who had constantly accompanied our army in the former war, and had obtained the privileges of a Roman citizen, and the rank of a knight,) took advantage of the general's indolence to perpetrate an act of atrocity, not unwisely judging that no man is more easily cut off than he who feels no fear, and that security is very frequently the commencement of calamity. He communicated his thoughts at first to a few, and afterwards to more, stating to them, and assuring them, that the Romans might be cut off by surprise; he then proceeded to add action to resolution, and fixed a time for carrying a plot into effect. Notice of his intention was given to Varus by Segestes, a man of that nation, worthy of credit, and of high rank; but fate was not to be opposed by warnings, and had already darkened the mental vision of the Roman general. Such, indeed, is the nature of things, that, in general, when the gods[94] design to reverse a man's good fortune, they perplex his thoughts, and, what is most distressing, make it appear that his sufferings happen to him through his own fault, so that accident is laid to the account of guilt. Varus refused to credit the information, asserting that he felt a trust in the good-will of the people, proportioned to his kindness towards them. However, after this first premonition, there was no time left for a second.

CXIX

The circumstances of this most dreadful calamity, than which none more grievous ever befel the Romans in a foreign country, since the destruction of Crassus in Parthia, I will endeavour to relate in my larger history, as has been done by others. At present we can only lament the whole. An army unrivalled in bravery, the flower of the Roman troops in discipline, vigour, and experience in war, was brought, through the supineness of its leader, the perfidy of the enemy, and the cruelty of Fortune, into a situation utterly desperate, (in which not even an opportunity was allowed the men of extricating themselves by fighting, as they wished, some being even severely punished by the general, for using Roman arms with Roman spirit,) and, hemmed in by woods, lakes, and bodies of the enemy in ambush, was entirely cut off by those foes whom they had ever before slaughtered like cattle, and of whose life and death the mercy or severity of the Romans had always been the arbitrator. The leader showed some spirit in dying, though none in fighting; for, imitating the example of his father and grandfather, he ran himself through with his sword. Of two prefects of the camp, Lucius Eggius gave as honourable an example of valour as Ceionius gave of baseness; for, after the sword had destroyed the greater part of the army, Ceionius advised a surrender, choosing to die by the hand of an executioner rather than in battle. Numonius Vala, a lieutenant-general under Varus, who in other cases conducted himself as a modest and well-meaning man, was, on this occasion, guilty of abominable treachery; for, leaving the infantry uncovered by the cavalry, he fled with the horse of the allies, and attempted to reach the Rhine. But Fortune took vengeance on his misdeed; for he did not survive his deserted countrymen, but perished in the act of desertion. The savage enemy mangled the half-burnt body of Varus; his head was cut off, and brought to Maroboduus, and being sent by him to Cæsar, was at length honoured with burial in the sepulchre of his family.

CXX

On receiving this intelligence, Cæsar hurried home to his father; and the constant patron of the Roman empire undertook its cause as usual. He was despatched to Germany, he secured the peace of Gaul, arranged the troops, fortified garrisons, and estimating himself by his own greatness, not by the confidence of the enemy who threatened Italy with an invasion like that of the Cimbri and Teutones, crossed the Rhine with his army. He thus made war upon a nation whom his father and his country would have been satisfied with keeping at a distance; he penetrated into the interior, opened roads, wasted the lands, burned the houses, overthrew all opposition, and then, with abundance of glory, and without losing a man of those who crossed the river, returned to winter quarters. Let due credit be given to Lucius Asprenas, who, serving as lieutenant-general under his uncle Varus, saved, by his manly and active exertions, a body of two legions which he commanded, from sharing in that dreadful calamity; and by going down speedily to the lower winter quarters, confirmed the allegiance of the nations on the hither side of the Rhine, which had now begun to waver. But some people, while they allow that he saved the living, are still of opinion, that he dishonestly possessed himself of the property of those slain with Varus, and, as far as he pleased, made himself the heir of the slaughtered army. The bravery of a prefect of the camp, too, named Lucius Cæditius, and of a party with him who were surrounded by a vast multitude of Germans at Alison, is much to be praised; for, by forming their plans with judgment, using vigilant foresight, and watching their opportunity, they surmounted difficulties which want rendered insupportable, and the force of the enemy almost insuperable, and opened for themselves with the sword a passage to their friends. Hence it is evident, that Varus, in other cases certainly a man of character and of good intentions, lost himself, and that noble army, rather through want of conduct in the commander, than through deficiency of courage in the soldiery. While the Germans were venting their rage on the prisoners, an act deserving of renown was performed by Cælius Caldus, a youth who did credit to his ancient family; he took hold of a part of the chains with which he was bound, and dashed it against his head with such force, that his blood and brains gushed out together, and he immediately expired.

CXXI

The same courage and good fortune which had animated Tiberius at the beginning of his command, still continued to attend him. After he had broken down the force of the enemy in various expeditions by land and sea, and had settled important affairs in Gaul, and composed, by coercion more than by punishment, the most violent commotions of the populace at Vienne; and after the senate and people of Rome, on a request being made by his father, that he might be invested with authority equal to his own in all the provinces and armies, had passed a decree to that effect, (for it would indeed have been unreasonable, if what he had secured should not be under his command, and if he, who was the first to bring succour, should not be thought entitled to a share of the honour,) he returned to Rome, and celebrated his triumph over Pannonia and Dalmatia, which had been long due to him, but had been deferred on account of the continuance of the wars. His triumph was magnificent, but who can be surprised at magnificence in a Cæsar? Who, however, will not admire the kindness of Fortune in this, that fame did not tell us, as was usual, that all the greatest leaders of the enemy were slain, but that the triumph displayed them to us in chains? On this occasion my brother and I had the happiness of accompanying him, among the most eminent personages, and those honoured with the principal distinctions.

CXXII

Among other instances in which the singular moderation of Tiberius Cæsar shines forth conspicuously, this claims our admiration, that although, beyond all doubt, he merited seven triumphs, he was yet satisfied with three. For who can doubt that, for reducing Armenia, fixing a king on its throne, (on whose head he placed the diadem with his own hand,) and for regulating the affairs of the east, he ought to have enjoyed a triumph? Or that, for his victories over the Rhæti and Vindelici, he deserved to enter the city in a triumphal car? And when, after his adoption, he exhausted the strength of Germany in three years of continued war, the same honour ought to have been offered him, and accepted by him. Again, after the disaster of the army of Varus, the rapid subjugation of the same Germany ought to have furnished a triumph for the same consummate general. But with respect to him you can hardly determine whether you should admire more his extraordinary exertions amid toil and danger, or his moderation with regard to honours.

CXXIII

We have now arrived at a period in which very great apprehension prevailed. For Augustus Cæsar, having sent his grandson Germanicus to finish the remainder of the war in Germany, and intending to send his son Tiberius into Illyricum, to settle in peace what he had subdued in war, proceeded with the latter into Campania, with the design of escorting him, and at the same time to be present at the exhibition of athletic sports, which the Neapolitans had resolved to give in honour of him. Although he had before this felt symptoms of debility and declining health, yet, as the vigour of his mind withstood them, he accompanied his son, and, parting from him at Beneventum, proceeded to Nola; where, finding that his health grew worse every day, and well knowing whose presence was requisite to the accomplishment of his wish to leave all things in safety after him, he hastily recalled his son, who hurried back to the father of his country, and arrived earlier than was expected. Augustus then declared that his mind was at ease; and being folded in the embrace of Tiberius, to whom he recommended the accomplishment of his father's views and his own, he resigned himself to die whenever the fates should ordain. He was in some degree revived by the sight and conversation of the person most dear to him; but the destinies soon overpowering every effort for his recovery, and his body resolving itself into its first principles, he restored to heaven his celestial spirit, in the seventy-sixth year of his age, and in the consulate of Pompey and Apuleius.

CXXIV

The universal apprehensions excited by this event; the alarm of the senate, the consternation of the people, the fears of the world, and the narrow line between safety and destruction on which we stood on that occasion, I have neither leisure to describe in this hasty narrative, nor can he, who has leisure, describe satisfactorily. One thing I can join with the voice of the public in declaring, that whereas we had dreaded the total ruin of the world, we did not perceive that it felt the slightest shock; and so powerful was the majesty of one man, that there was no occasion for arms, either to protect the good, or restrain the bad. Yet there was one struggle, as it may be called, in the state, between the senate and people of Rome on the one side, insisting on Cæsar's assuming his father's station, and himself on the other, desiring leave to stand on a level with his countrymen, instead of acting in the exalted character of a prince. At length he was overcome by reason, not by the attractions of honour; because he saw that whatever he did not take under his care would be lost. His case was singular in this, that he refused the sovereignty almost as long as others fought to obtain it. After he had seen his father restored to heaven, and had paid respect to his body with human, and to his name with Divine honours, the first act of his administration was the regulation of the elections, on a plan left by the deified Augustus in his own handwriting. At this time, my brother and I had the honour, as Cæsar's candidates[95], of being elected prætors, in the places next to men of the highest rank, and the priests; and we were remarkable in being the last recommended by Augustus, and the first by Tiberius Cæsar.

CXXV

The Commonwealth quickly reaped the fruit of its determination and its wish; and we soon learned what we must have suffered if that wish had not been complied with, and how greatly we had gained by its being fulfilled. For the army which was serving in Germany under the command of Germanicus, and the legions which were in Illyricum, being both seized at the same time with a kind of outrageous fury, and a violent passion for spreading universal disorder, demanded a new leader, a new constitution, a new republic; they even had the confidence to threaten that they would give laws to the senate, and to the prince; and they attempted to fix the amount of their pay, and the period of their service. They proceeded even to use their arms; the sword was drawn; and the impunity which was allowed them broke forth almost into the extremity of violence. They wanted, indeed, a head, to lead them against their country, but there were numbers ready to follow. However, the mature wisdom of the veteran emperor, who, refusing most of their demands, promised some indulgences without lowering his dignity, soon allayed and suppressed all these outrageous proceedings; severe vengeance being inflicted on the authors of the mutiny, and milder punishment on the rest. On this occasion, as Germanicus exerted his usual activity, so Drusus, who was sent by his father expressly to extinguish the flame of this military tumult, blazing, as it was, with enormous fury, enforced the ancient and primitive discipline, and by strong measures, though not without danger to himself[96], put a stop to those excesses, so pernicious both in the act and in the example; and reduced to obedience the soldiers that pressed around him, by the aid of the very swords with which he was beset. In these efforts he found an excellent assistant in Junius Blæsus, a man of whom it is difficult to decide whether his services were greater in the camp or in the camp. A few years after, being proconsul in Africa, he gained triumphal decorations, and the title of imperator. And being entrusted with the presidency of Spain, and the command of the army there, he was able, by his excellent abilities, and with the reputation which he had gained in the war with Illyricum, to keep the province in perfect peace and tranquillity; for while his fidelity to the emperor led him to adopt the most salutary measures, he had likewise ample authority to carry into execution what he planned. His care and fidelity were closely copied by Dolabella, a man of the noblest simplicity of character, when he commanded on the coast of Illyricum.

CXXVI

Of the transactions of the last sixteen years, which have passed in the view, and are fresh in the memory of all, who shall presume to give a full account? Cæsar deified his parent, not by arbitrary authority, but by paying a religious respect to his character. He did not call him a divinity, but made him one. In that time, credit has been restored to mercantile affairs, sedition has been banished from the forum, corruption from the Campus Martius, and discord from the senate-house; justice, equity, and industry, which had long lain buried in neglect, have been revived in the state; authority has been given to the magistrates, majesty to the senate, and solemnity to the courts of justice; the dissensions in the theatre[97] have been suppressed, and all men have either had a desire excited in them, or a necessity imposed on them, of acting with integrity. Virtuous acts are honoured, wicked deeds are punished. The humble respects the powerful, without dreading him; the powerful takes precedence of the humble without contemning him. When were provisions more moderate in price? When were the blessings of peace more abundant? Augustan peace, diffused over all the regions of the east and the west, and all that lies between the south and north, preserves every corner of the world free from all dread of predatory molestation. Fortuitous losses, not only of individuals, but of cities, the munificence of the prince is ready to relieve. The cities of Asia have been repaired; the provinces have been secured from the oppression of their governors. Honour promptly rewards the deserving, and the punishment of the guilty, if slow, is certain[98]. Interest gives place to justice, solicitation to merit. For the best of princes teaches his countrymen to act rightly by his own practice; and while he is the greatest in power, is still greater in example.

CXXVIII

It is seldom that men who have arrived at eminence, have not had powerful coadjutors in steering the course of their fortunes; thus the two Scipios had the two Lælii, whom they set in every respect on a level with themselves; thus the emperor Augustus had Marcus Agrippa, and after him Statilius Taurus. The newness of these men's families proved no obstruction to their attainment of many consulships and triumphs, and of sacerdotal offices in great numbers. For great affairs demand great co-operators; (in small matters[99], the smallness of assistance does not mar the proceedings;) and it is for the interest of the public, that what is necessary for business should be eminent in dignity, and that usefulness should be fortified with influence. In conformity with these examples, Tiberius Cæsar has had, and still has, Ælius Sejanus, a most excellent coadjutor in all the toils of government, a man whose father was chief of the equestrian order, and who on his mother's side is connected with some of the most illustrious and ancient families, ennobled by high preferments; who has brothers, cousins, and an uncle, of consular rank; who is remarkable for fidelity in the discharge of his duties, and for ability to endure fatigue, the constitution of his body corresponding with the vigour of his mind; a man of pleasing gravity, and of unaffected cheerfulness; appearing, in the despatch of business, like a man quite at ease; assuming nothing to himself, and hence receiving every honour; always deeming himself inferior to other men's estimation of him; calm in looks and conversation, but in mind indefatigably vigilant.

CXXVIII

In esteem for Sejanus's virtues, the judgment of the public has long vied with that of the prince. Nor is it at all new with the senate and people of Rome, to consider the most meritorious as the most noble. The man of old, before the first Punic war, three hundred years ago, exalted to the summit of dignity Titus Coruncanius, a man of no family, bestowing on him, beside other honours, the office of chief pontiff; they promoted Spurius Carvilius, a man of equestrian birth, and afterwards Marcus Cato, another new man, (not a native citizen, but born at Tusculum,) as well as Mummius Achaicus, to consulships, censorships, and triumphs. And they who considered Caius Marius, a man of the most obscure origin, as unquestionably the first in the Roman nation, before his sixth consulship; who had so high an esteem for Marcus Tullius, that he could obtain, almost by his sole recommendation, the highest offices for whomsoever he chose; and who refused nothing to Asinius Pollio, which men of the noblest birth had to obtain with infinite labour, were certainly of opinion that he who possessed the greatest virtues, was entitled to the greatest honours. The natural imitation of other men's examples led Cæsar to make trial of Sejanus, and occasioned Sejanus to bear a share of the burdens of the prince; and induced the senate and people of Rome cheerfully to call to the guardianship of their safety him whom they saw best qualified for the charge.

CXXIX

Having exhibited a general view of the administration of Tiberius Cæsar, let us now enumerate a few particulars respecting it. With what wisdom did he bring to Rome Rhascuporis, the murderer of Cotys, his own brother's son, and partner in the kingdom, employing in that affair the services of Pomponius Flaccus, a man of consular rank, naturally inclined to all that is honourable, and by pure virtue always meriting fame, but never eagerly pursuing it! With what solemnity as a senator and a judge, not as a prince, does he * * * hear[100] causes in person! How speedily did he crush * * *[101] when he became ungrateful, and attempted innovations! With what precepts did he form the mind of his Germanicus, and train him in the rudiments of war in his own camp, so that he afterwards hailed him the conqueror of Germany! What honours did he heap on him in his youth, the magnificence of his triumph corresponding to the grandeur of his exploits! How often has he honoured the people with donations! How readily has he, when he could do it with the sanction of the senate, supplied senators with property suitable to their rank, neither encouraging extravagance, nor suffering honourable poverty to be stripped of its dignity! In what an honourable style did he send his Germanicus to the transmarine provinces! With what energy, employing Drusus as a minister and coadjutor in his plans, did he force Maroboduus, who was clinging to the soil of the kingdom which he had possessed, to come forth, like a serpent concealed in the earth, (let me speak without offence to his majesty,) by the salutary charms of his counsels! How honourably, yet how far from negligently, does he keep watch over him! How formidable a war, excited by the Gallic chief Sacrovir and Julius Florus, did he suppress, and with such amazing expedition and energy, that the Roman people learned that they were conquerors, before they knew that they were at war, and the news of the victory outstripped the news of the danger! The African war too, perilous as it was, and daily increasing in strength, was quickly terminated under his auspices and direction.

CXXX

What structures has he erected in his own name, and those of his family! With what dutiful munificence, even exceeding belief, is he building a temple to his father! With how laudable a generosity of disposition is he repairing even the buildings of Cnæus Pompey, that were consumed by fire! Whatever has been at any time conspicuously great, he regards as his own, and under his protection. With what liberality has he at all times, and particularly at the recent fire on the Cælian Mount, repaired the losses of people of all conditions out of his own property! With what perfect ease to the public does he manage the raising of troops, a business of constant and extreme apprehension, without the consternation attendant on a levy! If either nature allows us, or the humility of man may take upon itself, to make a modest complaint of such things to the gods, what has he deserved that, in the first place, Drusus Libo should form his execrable plots; and, in the next, that Silius and Piso should follow his example, one of whom he raised to dignity, the other he promoted? That I may pass to greater matters, (though he accounted even these very great,) what has he deserved, that he should lose his sons in their youth, or his grandson by Drusus? But we have only spoken of causes for sorrow, we must now come to occasions of shame. With what violent griefs, Marcus Vinicius, has he felt his mind tortured in the last three years! How long has heart been consumed with affliction, and, what is most unhappy, such as he was obliged to conceal, while he was compelled to grieve, and to feel indignation and shame, at the conduct of his daughter-in-law[102] and his grandson[103]! And the sorrows of this period have been aggravated by the loss of his most excellent mother, a woman who resembled the gods more than human beings; and whose power no man ever felt but in the relief of distress or the conferring of honour.

CXXXI

Let our book be concluded with a prayer. O Jupiter Capitolinus, O Jupiter Stator! O Mars Gradivus, author of the Roman name! O Vesta, guardian of the eternal fire! O all ye deities who have exalted the present magnitude of the Roman empire to a position of supremacy over the world, guard, preserve, and protect, I entreat and conjure you, in the name of the Commonwealth, our present state, our present peace, [our present prince[104]!] And when he shall have completed a long course on earth, grant him successors to the remotest ages, and such as shall have abilities to support the empire of the world as powerfully as we have seen him support it! All the just designs of our countrymen * * * *

References
1 The former Scipio—the latter] The former was Scipio Africanus Major, the conqueror of Hannibal; the latter Scipio Africanus Minor, who destroyed Carthage and Numantia, and who is mentioned above, i., 15.
2 Before mentioned] See i., 2.
3 Shrinking from no penalty, &c.] Non recusando perduxit huc, &c. The text is here so obscure that Ruhnken says, "Ego nihil hic intelligo," and supposes that some words are lost. On Caudium, see Florus, i., 16.

4 II. All men were eager to secure a footing in the state] Omnibus statum concupiscentibus. Such is the way in which Krause and Orellius understand this phrase. Lipsius said that there was no sense in it, and conjectured omnibus (sc. legibus istis agrariis) statum concutientibus, which Gruter and Heinsius approved, and Ruhnken admitted into his text. But concupiscentibus seems to have been too hastily condemned by these critics. "Statum habere," says Krause, "est vel civitatem, vel bona certa, agros scilicet, habere, et sic esse aliquid in republicâ." So, he adds, the proscribed are said, c. 72, nullum statum habere.

5 IV. To whom Italy is but a stepmother] Quorum noverca est Italia. The idle and dissolute crowd that wandered the city, many of whom were not natives of the country, were not considered or valued by Italy as her children, but regarded by her with the disdain of a stepmother. The origin of the expression, as Wesseling has pointed out, is in Plato's Menexenus. Comp. Val. Max., vi., 2, 3.

6 With the head veiled] Velato capite. "Obvoluto capite elatus est, ne livor in ore appareret." Aurel. Vict., 58. This seems to have been customary.

7 VI. To transfer the privilege of being judges, &c.] See Pseudo-Sallust, first Epistle to Cæsar, c. 3, 8.

8 VIII. The sentence inclosed in brackets is evidently out of place, as Burman and Krause remark.

9 Eighteen sestertia] About 159l. 7s. 6d.

10 The Scipios] The office in which the Scipios were united was the ædileship, as Krause says, who supposes that some words to that effect have been lost out of the text.

11 IX. Of Ennius] The name of Ennius has been supplied in the texts of Ruhnken and Krause from a conjecture of Heinsius.

12 What he invented] He was an eminent writer of the Fabulæ Atellanæ, but not the inventor of that kind of composition. But perhaps he was the first that gave them any regularity of form.

13 X. Six sestertia] About 53l. 2s. 6d.

14 XI. Of strict temperance] Vitâ sanctus. This is, as Krause observes, evidently the sense. So Crassus, in c. 46, is said to be sanctissimus immunisque voluptatibus. Marius is called by Sallust, Jug., c. 63, lubidinis atque divitiarum victor.

15 XII. From some precaution of the fates] Ut præcaventibus fatis. As if the fates, by uniting them together at this time, had been anxious to prevent the discord that afterwards raged between them. Krause.

16 Curiæ were houses of assembly for the wards (curiæ) of the city.

17 XV. The words inclosed in brackets are entirely out of place, like those at the beginning of c. 8.

18 XVI. Assumption of the military dress] Ad saga iretur. "Livy, Epit. lxxii., says, with reference to these times, saga populus sumpsit. This military garment, the sagum, the Romans assumed, by a decree of the senate, in the most alarming wars, and retained it till better fortune appeared, when they returned to the toga. Compare Livy, Epit. lxxiv.; Cic., Phil., xiv., 1." Krause.

19 XVIII. Theophanes] A native of Mitylene, and friend of Pompey, of whose acts he wrote a history.

20 XIX. By a barbarian] Ab hoste. "A barbaro." Krause. Hostis, as opposed to civis.

21 XXI. To—the spectators] From the loss of their relatives.

22 XXII. With mortar] Calce arenâque. With lime and sand. Florus, iii., 21, says that Catulus died ignis haustu, by swallowing fire.

23 A reward—for his own destruction] Sui—periculi merces. "His property being divided among those who procured his death." Ruhnken.

24 XXIV. Procured a sentence of banishment] Aquâ ignique iis interdixit. See Florus, iii., 16.

25 XXV. Merciful to excess] Justissimo lenior. The text is here defective.

26 XXVI. A man of his father's spirit, though not of his father's length of life] Vir animi magis quam ævi paterni. "Ævum is here for ætas. Marius did not live as many years as his father, being killed young, as is related in c. 27." Krause.

27 The words at the end of this chapter are so defective, that it is useless to attempt a translation of them.

28 XXVII. Subterraneous passages] Cuniculos. "Made either for the conveyance of water, or for secret ways of exit from the city. See Strabo, v., p. 365." Krause.

29 XXVIII. A prize for depriving him of life] Quisque merces mortis suæ. Comp., c. 22.

30 XXX. Krause thinks there is a considerable hiatus between these two chapters.

31 Shameful death for himself] His treachery led to his desertion by his troops, and his defeat and death at the hands of Pompey. See Appian, B. C., i., 115; Plutarch, Sert., c. 27; Pomp., c. 20.

32 Rode through the city in his chariot] There was a law which forbade any one, who was not of consular or prætorian dignity, to have a triumph. But this was Pompey's second triumph. Hence Velleius says hoc quoque triumpho, "in this triumph also." See Plutarch, Pomp., c. 14, 22.

33 XXXII. Privilege of being judges] Judicandi munus. See the Pseudo-Sallust's First Epistle to Cæsar, c. 7.

34 Roscius Otho now restored] Otho Roscius—restituit. "The same word is twice used, in speaking of this law, by Cicero, pro Muræn., c. 19, so that it is probable, as Puteanus has suggested, that the equites had seats separate from the plebs before this well-known law was passed." Ruhnken.

35 Defeated the pirates * * * in various places] Prædonesque per multa * * * a multis locis, &c. A defective passage. The Bipont editor reads per multa maria multis, &c.

36 XXXIV. Noblest of new men] Novitatis nobilissimæ. The translation is Baker's.

37 Excelled in genius by those, &c.] Viz., by the Greeks.

38 XXXVI. A little before them, * * * Crassus, &c.] Anteaque * * * Crassum. Anteaque is a conjecture of Heinsius for saneque, the previous reading. Puteanus thinks that the name of Antonius is wanting in the text.

39 Rabirius] For Rabirius, Markland, Ep. Crit., p. 14, would read Varius. Perizonius thinks that Horatius should be inserted; and Burman supposes that the name of Propertius has dropped out of the text. But Velleius, says Krause, might have reasons for omitting both Horace and Propertius.

40 XL. Excepting the Parthian] "He means in the East. All other kings, except those of Parthia, owed their kingdoms to the indulgence of the Romans, and were subservient to their will, chiefly by the instrumentality of Pompey." Krause.

41 Excepting that of Paulus] Præterquam à Paullo. Vossius, Burman, Gruter, Ruhnken, and Krause concur in thinking these words spurious; for Pompey, according to Plutarch, Pomp., c. 45, brought into the treasury twenty thousand talents of gold and silver, a sum twice as great as that which was brought by Paulus Æmilius.

42 XLI. Watched him only with their eyes] They watched him only with their eyes, says Krause, having no mental communication with him. Had he made any alteration in his dress, they might have supposed that he was preparing for flight, and have laid hands upon him.

43 XLII. Envy—baseness of spirit] Sequebatur invidia inertiam. Oudendorp conjectured avaritia for invidia. Ruhnken justifies invidia by a sentence of Seneca, De Tranq. Anim., p. 345, ed. Gronov.: Alit enim livorem infelix inertia; et omnes destrui

cupiunt, quia se non poterunt provehere; and by another from Cicero, Phil., x., 1: Verum esse id quod ego semper sensi, neminem alterius, qui suæ consularet, virtuti invidere.

44 XLV. Sent into banishment] Aquâ et igni interdiceretur. See c. 24.

45 XLVI. A remarkable pair of consuls] Invictum par consulum. Invictum not being satisfactory, Lipsius and Heinsius conjectured inclitum par; Ruhnken unicum par. I have adopted the former.

46 Most atrocious crime] The assassination of Julius Caesar.

47 XLVIII. Ten thousand sestertia] Something more than 80,000l.

48 XLIX. Lentulus saw that his own security, &c.] "He was deeply in debt, from which he could not emerge as long as the state was undisturbed." Krause.

49 Kings, tetrarchs, and petty princes] Regumque et tetrarchum et dynastarum. See Sall., Cat., c. 20.

50 LII. Use a military expression—disband, &c.] The text is here corrupt and defective. Ruhnken ridicules the notion of dimitteret being the verbum militare, as most critics have supposed, and thinks that Velleius wrote something like this: Neque prius neque antiquius quicquam habuit quàm ut in omnes partes præcones clamantes, parce civibus, ut militari et verbo et consuetudine utar, dimitteret. For a confirmation of this conjecture he refers to Appian, B. C., ii., p. 783; Suet. Cæs., c. 75; Flor., iv., 2. The translation which I have given is borrowed from Baker.

51 LVI. Acanthus wood] Acantho. The acanthus was a tree of the acacia kind, now generally supposed to be the same as the Mimosa Nilotica of Linnæus, or "Egyptian thorn." See Plin., H. N., xxiv., 12; Miller's Gardener's Dict., Art. Acacia; Martyn on Virg. Georg., ii., 119.

52 Tortoise-shell] "We must suppose that the fercula, or frames on which the articles were carried in the procession, were inlaid with tortoise-shell, as is now the case with many articles of furniture." Krause.

53 Six hundred thousand sestertia] Something more than 4,800,000l.

54 LIX. He himself has anticipated me] Prævenit, et * * * * &c. "Vossius and Bœcler rightly refer prævenit to Augustus himself, and his commentaries on his life mentioned by Suetonius, Aug., c. 2." Krause. Some words, which introduce the account of Octavius's father, have been lost.

55 The orb of the sun—regularly curved, &c.] Solis orbis—curvatus æqualiter rotundatusque, in colorem arcûs. It is not possible to explain these words at all satisfactorily. Suetonius, in speaking of the same occurrence, Aug., c. 95, says, circulus ad speciem cælestis arcûs orbem solis ambiit; and Seneca, Q. N., i., 2; Dion Cassius, xlv., 4; and Plin., H. N., ii., 28, allude to the matter in a similar way. Hence Hottinger, a friend of Herelius, conjectured that we should read curvatunt æqualiter rotundatumque versicolorem arcum, &c.

56 LX. Seven hundred thousand sestertia] Something more than 5,650,000l.

57 False insertions—in Cæsar's registers] Actorum ejusdem insertis falsis, civitatibusque * * * corrupti commentarii. I have omitted the last three words. Various emendations of the passage have been suggested, but to little purpose.

58 LXII. Laudandus et tollendus] The play on the word tollendus cannot be rendered. Tollo means not only to raise or extol, but to take out of the way. It is as if we should say of a man that merits hanging, that he deserves to be exalted.

59 LXV. To revenge a father, &c.] It was more incumbent on Octavius to revenge the death of Julius Cæsar than on Antony; Cæsar being his adopted son, Antony only his friend.

60 LXVII. Germans, (that is, brothers,) &c.] De Germanis. A play on the Latin word Germanus.

61 LXXII. Whom we lately saw] Nuper à nobis visi. He had died a little before.

62 No position in the state] Nullum habentibus statum. See note on ii., 2.

63 LXXIII. A freedman among his own freedmen] Libertorum suorum libertus. He lowered himself, and laid himself under obligations to them.

64 LXXV. Daughter] By adoption into the Julian family according to the will of Augustus. Tacit. Ann., i., 8; Suet. Aug., 101.

65 LXXVII. In his own Carinæ] In Carinis suis. A pun on carinæ, ships, which was also the name of an open place, or street, in Rome. Romanoque foro et lautis mugire Carinis. Virg. Æn., viii., 361.

66 LXXXI. Twelve hundred sestertia] About 10,000l.

67 LXXXII. The commencement of this chapter, in which Krause retains the old, unintelligible reading, is translated according to the emendation of Ruhnken: Quâ æstate Cæsar tam prospere sepelivit in Siciliâ bellum, fortuna in Cæsare et republicâ mutavit ad Orientem. This is the best of all the corrections that have been proposed; though the words in Cæsare et republicâ, as a Gottingen reviewer observes, (Ephem. Lit., 1799, p. 120,) will hardly satisfy every reader.

68 LXXXIV. Amyntas] The successor of Deiotarus in the kingdom of Galatia.

69 Dellius] Quintus Dellius, to whom Horace addresses Od. ii., 3. He deserted from Dolabella to Cassius, from Cassius to Antony, and from Antony to Cæsar. Sen. Suasor., i. The text is here imperfect, and a few words are omitted in the translation.

70 By her name] Nomine. Not saluting her as a queen, but calling her merely Cleopatra.

71 LXXXVIII. Fully contented with the narrow purple] The text has angusti clavi pene contentus, which is manifestly corrupt, for any trustworthy example of contentus with a genitive is not to be found. Ruhnken thinks that pene is a corruption of some substantive. The Basil editor gives angusto clavo. For pene, Krause proposes bene or planè. The angustus clavus was the badge of a knight.

72 Calpurnia—mentioned above] See c. 26.

73 XCII. By primitive strictness and the greatest firmness of mind] Priscâ severitate et summâ constantiâ. The words which follow these, vetere consulum more ac severitate, are not translated, being, as Krause observes, a manifest interpolation.

74 XCIV. Artavasdes, &c.] There is here a hiatus in the text. The words in brackets are a suggestion of Lipsius.

75 XCVII. Unassuming demeanour] Par sui æstimatio. "Just estimation of himself."

76 C. Julius Antonius] Son of Mark Antony, by Fulvia.

77 CIII. That he was all in all to every one] Quàm in illo [omnia] omnibus fuerint. "How much all things were in him for all." The omnia is an insertion of Krause's, borrowed by him from Lipsius's conjecture, quàm ille omnia omnibus fuerit.

78 CV. Lupia] Now called Lippe; a river of Westphalia, rising in the bishopric of Paderborn, and running into the Rhine near Wesel.

79 CX. At the place already mentioned] In prædicto loco. Apparently Carnuntum, c. 109, fin.

80 A vast number of soldiers] Magnus numerus vexillariorum. What the vexillarii were, is not quite certain. Ernesti, in his Excursus on the subject, subjoined to Tacitus's History, thinks that they were tirones, and the same as the hastati.

81 CXI. With the tribunes of the people elect] Designatis tribunis plebis. According to Lipsius, the tribunes of the people were at this period chosen only from the senators. If so, some particular favour was shown to Velleius on this occasion, allowing him, though not yet a senator, to stand on an equality with the tribunes.

82 In my quæstorship, &c.] After taking the detachment of the army into Germany, says Krause, Velleius seems to have returned to Rome to enter upon his quæstorship; and then, during the time that he held that office, to have been again despatched to

Germany by Augustus in the quality of legate, without waiting to take a province at the expiration of his quæstorship.

83 Did we behold] Vidimus. Krause's text has fudimus, a conjecture of Heinsius. Burman holds to vidimus, as savouring less of boastfulness.

84 With what attention, &c.] The text is here mutilated and obscure.

85 CXII. At the standards of the legions] Apud signa—legionum. Krause takes signa for interior acies. Is apud signa the same as apud vexillarios, in Ernesti's sense of vexillarii? See note on c. 110.

86 Agrippa] See [#CIV | c. 104]], init.

87 Also his grandfather] An inadvertent repetition; "natural grandfather" occurring above.

88 CXIII. Siscia] In Pannonia, now Sisseck, at the confluence of the Save and Colapis.

89 CXIV. On horseback] "Not in any carriage, or lectica." Ruhnken.

90 Sat at meals] Cænavit sedens. Not reclining on a couch.

91 CXVI. A surname for his son] He left to his son the surname Gætulicus.

92 CXVII. Arrived] The verb is wanting in the original, as well as the words inclosed in brackets below, which are suggested by Vossius.

93 Nothing human but the voice, &c.] "He thought them mere brutes, and therefore undertook their transformation into men." Krause.

94 CXVIII. When the gods, &c.] A repetition of the sentiment at the end of c. 57.

95 CXXIV. Cæsar's candidates] Candidatis Cæsaris. That is, brought forward and recommended by Cæsar. See Suet. Aug., c. 56; Quintil., vi., 3.

96 CXXV. Not without danger to himself] Ancipitia sibi. These words are in some way corrupt; and the sentence is otherwise defective.

97 CXXVI. Dissensions in the theatre] These were not of so small importance as might be supposed, being sometimes attended with great bloodshed. See Suet. Tib., c. 57; Tacit. Ann., i., 77.

98 If slow, is certain] Sera, sed aliqua. Lipsius would read sed æqua, but Gruter and others think that aliqua may be right; i.e. some punishment is sure to follow.

99 CXXVII. In small matters, &c.] "If the words be Velleius's, the observation is trifling, and utterly unworthy of him." Krause.

100 CXXIX. Does he * * * hear] Pressius audit. The word pressius, which can hardly be sound, though Perizonius tries to defend it, I have not attempted to translate.

101 Did he crush * * *] Whose name should fill this blank is doubtful. Krause thinks that of Archelaus, king of Cappadocia.

102 CXXX. Daughter-in-law] Agrippina, the wife of Germanicus.

103 Grandson] Nero, the son of Germanicus. Velleius merely echoes the calumnies of Tiberius on both these characters.

104 CXXXI. [Our present prince!] The words hunc principem, which the text requires, are supplied from a conjecture of Lipsius. The conclusion of the prayer is imperfect.

Note from the Editor

Odin's Library Classics strives to bring you unedited and unabridged works of classical literature. As such this is the complete and unabridged version of the original English text. The English language has evolved since the writing and some of the words appear in their original form, or at least the most commonly used form at the time. This is done to protect the original intent of the author. If at any time you are unsure of the meaning of a word, please do your research on the etymology of that word. It is important to preserve the history of the English language.

Taylor Anderson

Printed in Great Britain
by Amazon